anyone who's anyone

HARPER

An Imprint of HarperCollins*Publishers*

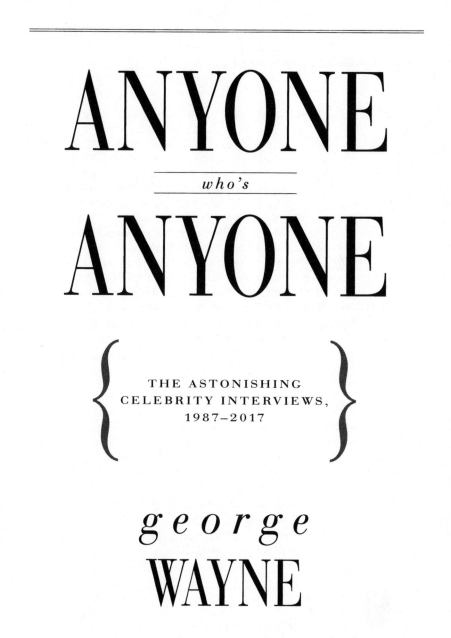

ANYONE

who's

ANYONE

$\Big\{$ THE ASTONISHING
CELEBRITY INTERVIEWS,
1987–2017 $\Big\}$

george

WAYNE

Vanity Fair is © and TM Condé Nast. Interviews used with permission: Cindy Adams (February 2003); Dennis Basso (May 2004); Milton Berle (February 1994); Mr. Blackwell (May 1995); David Copperfield (February 1996 & November 2012); Tony Curtis (June 2002); Carrie Donovan (August 1998); Robert Evans (April 1999); Fabio (November 1992); Farrah Fawcett (October 2000); Sarah Ferguson; Duchess of York (May 2000); Carrie Fisher (November 2006); Helen Gurley Brown (June 2000); Bridget Hall (December 1995); Jerry Hall (May 1997); Charlton Heston (September 1994); Philip Johnson (November 1998); Eartha Kitt (June 2001); Kenneth Jay Lane (November 1996); Dolph Lundgren (June 1995); Kate Moss (January 1994); LeRoy Neiman (August 1996); Régine (September 1996); Debbie Reynolds (February 1997); Geraldo Rivera (June 1997); Joan Rivers (March 2004); Francesco Scavullo (October 1997); Russell Simmons (October 2003); Martha Stewart (October 1994); Ivana Trump (October 1993); Ivanka Trump (June 2008); Kathleen Turner (April 2002); Donatella Versace (March 1994); Barry White (November 1999).

Interviews reprinted with permission, courtesy of *The Daily Front Row*: Ross Bleckner, Graydon Carter, Jackie Collins, and Anna Wintour.

Interview reprinted with permission, courtesy of *R.O.M.E.*: Sandra Bernhard, Bob Colacello, Marc Jacobs, Prince Federico Pignatelli della Leonessa, Tamara Mellon, Ian Schrager.

All illustrations © 2016, Laura Baran

HarperCollins books may be purchased for educational, business, or sales promotional use. For information, please email the Special Markets Department at SPsales@harpercollins.com.

FIRST EDITION

Designed by William Ruoto

Library of Congress Cataloging-in-Publication Data has been applied for.

ISBN 978-0-06-238007-4

17 18 19 20 21   RRD   10 9 8 7 6 5 4 3 2 1

This particular bit of genius is
dedicated to Gem & Frenchy . . .
Mum & Dad

Phillip, Janice, and Debra . . .
brother and sisters.

{ CONTENTS }

CONTENTS

CONTENTS

{ FOREWORD }

George Wayne and I arrived in New York about the same time. I came from Canada in the seventies, to write for *Time* magazine and valiantly tried to look like I belonged there. George came from Jamaica in the eighties to peer into the Mudd Club and almost immediately began looking like he belonged there. He learned quickly that writing about powerful people had a way of earning him, if not exactly their respect, then at least their attention. To this end he founded a magazine, which he called *R.O.M.E.* It was a deliriously lo-fi affair that leaned heavily on collage and might well have been called O.P.X.M.—Other People's Xerox Machines. It might help for you to imagine the Internet on paper, photocopied and stapled together by the proprietor himself. Long before it was fashionable to cultivate a high-low sensibility, George was pioneering his with *R.O.M.E.* Society fixtures such as Jackie Kennedy and Lynn

Wyatt shared pages with drag queens and club kids. Lists predominated. There was a lot of Andy Warhol and Grace Jones. With a circulation verging on three figures, he could afford to play fast and loose with the clearance of rights.

At the offices of *Spy*, which my fellow editor Kurt Andersen and I founded in the mid-eighties, George was a fixture. (I do recall that we went through a lot of copy paper on those days when George was hanging around the office.) Not a week, and sometimes not a day, went by when he didn't ask me for a job. For five years I politely rebuffed his advances. Then, on a hot July morning in Paris, a year or so after I had gravitated to *Vanity Fair*, I bumped into him outside a Karl Lagerfeld show. He was sitting on one of those stone stanchions outside the Louvre. He casually asked me for a job. It had become his form of greeting me and this time he said it more out of rote than with any conviction. And for one reason or another—an admiration for his tenacity, or perhaps the mild Parisian morning air—I said, "Oh what the hell," and gave him one.

We thought it safer to keep him in the Q&A silo of magazine writing. He accepted the proposition and George's "column" in *Vanity Fair* just sort of took off. To be on the office floor with him was to submit to the state of chaos that tends to swirl permanently around writers and photographers of talent—or just those who are magnets for disorder. Someone's apartment was always on fire (occasionally his). Someone was always drumming up or rehashing or resuming a blood feud (often with him). Someone was always storming out of an interview (almost always with him).

Outrage over the style in which George conducted his notorious Q&As was not uncommon. No topic was off-limits; on the contrary, the more off-limits the subject, the more it became the topic. "We have to be a little controversial," he declared in one Q&A, "or what's the point?" In the analog days, before the famous took to blogs and Twitter to catalogue their wounded sensibilities, they wrote letters to the editor (or had their lawyers write them), and I received more than a few on the subject of George's Q&As. What George never bothered to explain was that the mild but real indignities of fame—autograph seekers interrupting meals, humiliating casting calls, the day the scripts stop showing up—were actually worse than the mischief he would create during an interview that the subject had consented to with eyes wide open. And with George there was never any question about what you were getting into. If you knew the game he was playing, you could play along, and after the initial shock wore off, you could be as candid as you liked and still come across as a pillar of discretion.

In an age when pop stars and spin-class addicts earnestly refer to themselves as "survivors," George is authentically a member of that class. If you were gay and black and stylish in New York in the 1980s, the outlook ahead was anything but guaranteed: you weren't exactly setting money aside in a 401(k). The "Downtown" that George celebrated for decades has been recast and repaved for the stroller set, and as long-term leases expired, the corner newsstand where *R.O.M.E.* was sold made way for an ATM, then a Starbucks, and finally a vacant, glass-walled high-rise. George is still in his apartment in Greenwich Village, still taking your measure from behind his ever-present sunglasses, and still reminding us that we could all use a bit more mischief in our lives before the age of the individual passes us by for good.

— Graydon Carter

anyone who's anyone

G W definitely believes that *People* magazine is the reason for it. *People* is the reason I live in New York City, and the reason I've become a carnivore of pop culture.

The first time I lay my hands on a copy of the magazine, I was a skinny fifteen-year-old growing up on the British West Indian island of Jamaica. The nurse at the elitist West Indian boys' boarding school I attended, Munro College (or "Jamaica's Eton," as people often refer to it) in Malvern, was the one who introduced me to the glossy American weekly; it was my first taste of the documentation of celebrity culture. And it was at that moment, circa 1978, that I began to realize my life's calling. For this shy, insecure boy in the bushes of Jamaica, the faraway world of *People*—Brooke Shields, Andy Warhol, Truman Capote—was something foreign and exotic to fantasize about.

In Arce Sitam Quis Occultabit: "A City Set on a Hill Cannot Be Hid." So went the motto for Munro College. Our illustrious headmaster, Richard Roper, would never let us forget how privileged we were to be part of a citadel that had groomed young men for more than 122 years and produced more Rhodes Scholars than any other institution in the West Indies. All Munro boys were reminded every day of our academic lineage when we gathered in the dining hall for the three daily prison-like rations—looming oil portraits and Hall of Fame rosters of famous Munronians from the beginning of the twentieth century lined the walls.

Acclimatizing to the rigors of boarding school was a particularly difficult task for me. I came from a rather . . . well-to-do upbringing, so living in the cold, creaking, aged dormitories and sleeping on a tiny worn-thin mattress for seven years took a lot of getting used to. Dealing with bullies, cold showers, khaki uniforms, and the daily prayer at the crack of dawn in the school chapel was awful. Besides, GW was not blessed with the physical prowess or the necessary gung-ho jock mentality to survive in such an austere place. No, boarding school did not help the self-esteem of the young GW, and so he spent much of his free time in the living room of the nurse's rather chic quarters reading *People* magazine. That was far more interesting than, say, getting his shins banged up on the hockey field. Or being forced to don white flannel and play that stupid game of cricket.

The last three years of boarding school were the toughest. But they also turned out to be the prime of GW's life.

Something began to bloom. . . . The shy, nervous, often-perplexed, unhappy, skinny little boy was beginning to come into his own.

The Jamaica Broadcasting Corporation (JBC), at the time the only television station in Jamaica, had somehow managed to produce a wildly popular trivia show called *Schools' Challenge Quiz*, in which "quiz bowl" teams from the leading high schools across Jamaica would compete against one another during weekly live broadcasts. In no time, *Schools' Challenge Quiz* had grown to become the most watched television program in Jamaican history, what with the jangled nerves of the contestants and the exciting, nail-biting tension (many a match went to the final buzzer). The entire nation would gather before their TV sets on Tuesday nights to watch the broadcast, waiting to see who would be knocked out of the competition and who would move on. The two Jamaican high schools with the most astute quartet of general-knowledge superstars would square off in the grand finale.

Being on the Munro College Quiz Team certainly rivaled being a star jock. The school's football (Americans say soccer) team was steeped in glorious history, and they were definitely considered the school's superstars, the campus elite (along with the cricket players and, to some extent, track-and-field athletes). But still, being one of the four members of the prestigious Quiz Team was like being thrust into the stratosphere.

It was the "den mother" school nurse who actually suggested that GW try out for Munro's much-revered Quiz

Team, and I made the cut. My specialties were English literature, current affairs, and film. The two seasons that GW was a member of the Munro College Quiz Team (1977–78, 1978–79), the school was in the finals. Enough said. The campus wimp had somehow evolved into the campus celebrity. Fan mail was pouring in from across the country; suddenly every jock superstar on campus wanted to be best friends with GW. I surprised myself with how much I enjoyed the glare of live television lights and the ensuing rapture from the general populace that accompanied being a TV star.

The first year we were in the finals of the JBC *Schools' Challenge Quiz*, this budding TV star found himself emboldened by the sudden attention of one particular campus jock. It was a bewildering time, and it became increasingly difficult for GW to fathom what was happening as his affection for the jock grew, and vice versa. Sexual curiosity was rampant, and GW was more than intrigued with the notion of exploring man-to-man sexual tendencies.

One must keep in mind that homosexuality was a greater taboo in Jamaica than in even the ultra-conservative, Bible-thumping parts of the United States. And to even declare that those boy-to-boy peccadilloes were unquestionably some of GW's fondest memories of growing up in a Jamaican boarding school would undeniably cause a monumental jaw-dropping reaction from sea to shining sea across the Caribbean. Oh well.

From the love affair with that incredibly hot jock, GW went on to experience something quite similar with one of the leading professional athletes on the island of Jamaica. And that, too, was unforgettable. By the end of the second consecutive appearance in the quiz bowl finals, GW was well versed in the art of having a jock-boy love affair. The last two years as a Munronian afforded me some of the most cherished encounters of male bonding.

The year 1979 quickly became one of GW's best ever. Not only did Munro College win the JBC *Schools' Challenge Quiz*, but GW won the individual prize given for the English literature category. The welcome we received back at the city set on a hill after we'd been victorious was a sight to see: it was almost like a New York welcome for the pennant-winning Yankees. On top of all that, GW surprised everyone, most of all himself, by passing all four Cambridge International Examinations–Advanced Level and being accepted to the University of Georgia in Athens. The American adventure was about to unfold.

Nothing could have prepared GW for the culture shock of a small, Southern college town. My freshman-year roommate, one big, blond surfer mastodon from New Jersey, whose name GW feels no need to recall, was the ultimate embodiment of the word "primate." Every morning, for one solid year, GW was roused from his slumber by the blazing boombox anthems of Bruce Springsteen. And most every night, the poor GW was forced to deal with trying to sleep while listening to the groaning and the grunting from the small bed a mere few feet away as the primate plowed his assortment of bimbos into ecstatic oblivion. This was not at all what GW had expected his new life in America to be all about.

The separation of races and the cliques fueled by the fraternity and sorority life at the University of Georgia were also troubling. For foreign students it was doubly hard to fit in. But GW has long lived by the adage "When in Rome, do as the Romans do." And if Athens, Georgia, did one thing well, it was to hone GW's "downtown sensibility." The city was ripe with beatnik creativity, and had one of the strongest, most influential underground music scenes in the country. The B-52s were just about to head off to New York City (and international stardom) when GW arrived in town. R.E.M. was still a local garage band, wowing us all with free concerts on Legion Field. Pylon and Love Tractor, also hip, well-known bands out of Athens, could be found on any given night at the legendary 40 Watt Club. The scene was very postmodern Haight-Ashbury.

When I wasn't exploring the Atlanta scene or toying with the insipid food in the college's Bolton Hall cafeteria, I was treading through the latest copies of *People* and *Interview* magazines, daydreaming about living in New York City, hanging out with Andy Warhol and Truman Capote, and editing my very own magazine, which I'd name *Rome*. A dear friend of mine, Mark Thomas, suggested that *Rome* become *R.O.M.E.*, standing for "Revelers of My Ego." The seed was planted. As luck would have it, in early 1982, the college led a group of around twelve seniors on an exploratory trip to New York City. Fate determined that we would stay in the Roosevelt Hotel, almost right across from 350 Madison Avenue, then the hallowed home of glossy magazine conglomerate Condé

Nast. GW was smitten; he knew he had no alternative but to move to New York City.

And so, in the winter of 1984, armed with a Southern college degree in journalism, GW bought a one-way ticket from Hartsfield to LaGuardia. The Eastern Airlines 727 arrived in New York without the plane losing an engine or any of its skin, which in itself was a major feat for Eastern Airlines at the time.

My first jobs in New York City were in the advertising industry, where I was first a glorified secretary to the creative director on the fabulous, newly acquired J. C. Penney account at N. W. Ayer, and then a junior copywriter, before joining UniWorld Group, the leading African-American advertising agency at the time. At UniWorld, GW busted butt on the Burger King, RCA, and Coors beer accounts. He hated each and every minute of the corporate culture, and the phony world of the advertising business. He prayed to be fired, and soon his prayers were answered.

GW, happily armed with a green card, loved America even more when he realized that being on unemployment meant that he still got paid for six months! Those unemployment checks meant that GW could fully immerse himself in the full-time pursuit of one of his life's goals: becoming best friends with Andy Warhol. Living in the hip East Village in a one-bedroom apartment share, GW spent his days trying to meet with all the cool editors at magazines like *Spy* and *New York Talk*, and at night he would roam the social whirl of Gotham. He finally met Andy Warhol for the first time at the Puck Building on Lafayette Street. Andy's hand was clammy, but he was very nice. And GW will never forget self-proclaimed downtown curator Baird Jones graciously spouting, "George Wayne is genius, Andy." Andy wasn't impressed, but that was okay.

No matter how hard I tried, no one at those snobby downtown magazines would give GW any writing jobs because, well, I had no clips, no published work to show. That's when I decided it was time to compile all those fabulous story ideas bouncing around in my head and bring my own magazine to life. And so, in 1986, *R.O.M.E.* was born. GW cut, pasted, laid out, and Xeroxed about sixty copies. They sold out at four dollars apiece. GW had no idea that he was about to lead a movement, a revolution, but *R.O.M.E.* was an undeniable hit from the day it was born. An instant hit which found an immediate audience—my little homemade Xeroxed magazine! Before there was *Wallpaper*, before there was *Visionaire*, before there was *Joe*, there was *R.O.M.E.* By the time the fifth volume of *R.O.M.E.* appeared in the early 1990s, Karl Lagerfeld, LeRoy Neiman, Isaac Mizrahi, Azzedine Alaïa, Alex Katz, Steven Meisel, Graydon Carter—leading image makers of the time—had become major fans.

Then one day the savvy magazine editor David Hershkovits, who founded the downtown magazine *Paper*, bought a copy of *R.O.M.E.*, took it home, read it, and decided to track down this George Wayne person. GW considers the day he landed in the *Paper* magazine offices on lower Broadway a benchmark moment: David Hershkovits offered George

Wayne his own column. GW was now truly the arbiter he had always considered himself to be.

It was shortly after that when GW fulfilled yet another dream: working at *Interview* magazine. Ingrid Sischy was the new editor in chief; GW was hired as assistant editor to Ingrid's second-in-command at the time, Glenn O'Brien. And wow, what a crazy time that was. Given all the out-of-control egos in that office, GW soon begged Ingrid Sischy to offer him a contributing editor role, a position that she granted and which he holds to this day on the *Interview* masthead. *Interview*, of course, is known for the art of the interview, and it was in this arena that GW realized his extra-deft mastery of the celebrity question-and-answer format. He conducted one of the first interviews in America with the newly arrived model ingénue Naomi Campbell, which sparked a media frenzy (and a tempestuous relationship with Naomi Campbell, which also continues to this day).

One of the remarkable things GW found as he continued to produce each and every monumental issue of *R.O.M.E.* was how easy it was to find the right, receptive magazine sellers to help peddle his one-of-a-kind, avant-garde journal. But one person in particular stands out as a godsend: Margit Larsen, the legendary magazine-stand czarina at the old Condé Nast building. She was always there with support, always calling up GW and informing him when an important editor or Condé Nast chieftain bought an issue of *R.O.M.E.* One day Margit called "Lilliput," the *R.O.M.E.* headquarters (and tiny GW residence in the historic West Village), and hissed excitedly in that guttural German tongue of hers, "Si [Newhouse, the ruler of the revered Condé Nast magazine empire] just bought two issues of *R.O.M.E.*!" She paused. "Vell?! Aren't you excited?"

GW was beyond excited. The year was 1991, and it was because of that news from Margit Larsen that he worked up the courage to pen a memorandum to Emperor Si, basically listing ten reasons why he ought to buy *R.O.M.E.* and become a supreme, truly acknowledged patron of the arts. A few days after the letter was mailed, GW got a phone call from a woman by the name of Linda Wells, asking him to come into her office. She was currently all the talk of the glossy magazine industry because Emperor Si had decided to launch her as his next megastar editrix; he handed her the reins to a brand-new magazine for women about beauty, which, of course, turned out to be *Allure*. When GW went to meet her, Linda told me point-blank that she wanted me as an exclusive contributing editor to *Allure* magazine, and offered me a fat and juicy Condé Nast contract to go with the title. I almost fell off my chair.

That was unquestionably the happiest day of my life since my arrival in New York City. GW was well aware that this was Emperor Si Newhouse's way of trying to help support the craft of George Wayne. And GW also knew that being one of the first writers recruited to help create the prototype, the DNA, of this new *Allure* was a tremendous challenge and amazing opportunity. GW's first assignment was to visit the chic Caribbean island of St. Barthélemy during the height of the winter season. Can you imagine? Thirteen days in St. Barts—thirteen days under the auspices of *Allure* magazine—spending Christmas 1992 with Quincy Jones, Martha Stewart, Anna Wintour, Herb Ross and Lee Radziwill, Diane von Furstenberg, and other such stellar members of the glamorama. What about the second assignment? What could possibly top that trip to St. Barts? Well, the editor in chief decided that GW ought to scour Paris during the height of the supermodel era and the October prêt-à-porter season. Needless to say, those first four years were the *gloria-in-excelsis* years.

The year 1992 was without a doubt the most significant of the nine years since the arrival of this Jamaican in New York, and not only because of the amazing *Allure* position. It was a year when the brand name *R.O.M.E.* made international headlines, linking forever the names George Wayne and Claudia Schiffer when the German fräulein lobbed a thirty-million-dollar lawsuit in the lap of the magazine. The ice maiden of the catwalk was furious that *R.O.M.E.* volume VI had featured a tongue-in-cheek series of photos of her topless as she changed backstage at a Chanel fashion show in New York City. It was the first time that any publication had ever featured any intimate part of Claudia Schiffer's body. And she went ballistic. The *R.O.M.E. v.* Claudia Schiffer lawsuit made the front page of the London *Times* and every major daily from Sydney, Australia, to Bonn, Germany. It would be total misinformation for GW to declare that I was not a stressed-out, nervous wreck at the time of the lawsuit. (In hindsight, I'm tremendously disappointed that I didn't seize the moment and milk the publicity wheel for all that scandal was worth.) God is great, however: the lawsuit was resolved without *R.O.M.E.* forfeiting a penny to the outstretched palm of Claudia Schiffer.

All this GW talk wasn't lost on the brilliantly astute, newly appointed editor in chief of *Vanity Fair*, Graydon Carter, who soon offered GW the dream gig he so craved. And so the GW celebrity Q&A column for *Vanity Fair* was born. It's become an institution for the Vanities section of the Condé Nast jewel in the crown. There are well-read people all over the globe who "get," who understand, the philosophy of George Wayne. And that is why, we truly believe, they will be quite thrilled to learn of GW's pièce de résistance: this collection of my absolute favorite GW Q&A columns. Here they are in all their glory. Published as one for the very first time. The dates atop the interviews indicate the month and year they were actually published. What now follows is a truly original update of my oral history with celebrity. These are clearly not all of my celebrity interview encounters, but are unquestionably some of the most cherished and memorable.

{ JOAN RIVERS }

MARCH 2004

J oan is now with her beloved Edgar in that iCloud heaven somewhere over the rainbow, but New Yorkers especially will always hold a revered place in their hearts for Joan Rivers. The last time I saw Joan Rivers in the flesh was on November 28, 2013. I was walking on the street where she lived in the rarified air there in the Fifties between Fifth Avenue and Madison Avenue of New York City when she spotted me way before I noticed her. By the time I realized who it was, we were touching cheeks as she squealed, "You look exactly the same as the day I met you!" She was still as sharp as a tack, this legend, and clearly enjoying each and every moment of her resurgence and pop culture relevance. She asked me where I was going. I told her just around the corner to one of my favorite restaurants in the world, which is Nello, to have some squid ink pasta alone on the eve of my birthday. She didn't flinch and told me to keep in touch as she scribbled her private email address.

But my most unforgettable memory was the day I went shopping with Joan Rivers at Barneys. A trip to Nepal was on her agenda, and she was looking for a fashionable anorak to help her contend with the chill of the Himalayas. Not that Joan Rivers needed any excuse to go shopping. I remember going to her vast Manhattan apartment and immediately noticing the pincushion in her sitting room—I Shop Therefore I Am, it read. Going shopping with Joan was like nothing I had ever experienced. It involved a full-on entourage, not just the stylist, but the hairdresser, the makeup artist, the business manager, and yes, her pet-a-pouf Spike Rivers (her beloved Yorkshire terrier).

"I haven't got time like these ladies to go to the spa or to the beauty shop," she said in that signature hoarse voice of hers.

"Everything I do, I do on the run. I always shop on tour. I'll have a day in Houston where I just bought a wonderful white suit. I'll have a day in Toronto where I got a great scarf. Barneys gives me my basics."

Of course, the topic soon strayed to plastic surgery. "I was never the pretty girl—ever. But I've done no more [surgery] than the Chers or Carol Burnetts. I haven't had my eyes changed. I haven't had my nose fixed or my teeth replaced. I haven't had my boobs done. I haven't had a chin implant. I haven't had my arms thinned—and my ass has not been filled! Jane Fonda, for all that talk about health and vegetables—she was eating them on the way to the plastic surgeon."

That may be so, but I also so fondly recall attending a 7:00 p.m. fashion show in February 2011, where Joan was sitting in the front row of Elie Tahari during New York Fashion Week. And as we air kissed and I made my way to my seat, I couldn't help but think to myself that her face was pulled tighter than the sail of a Larry Ellison America's Cup yacht. We did this interview at her apartment seven years before I saw her perched in that front row. And she was, and will always be, the indefatigable Joan. . . .

GW: So, darling—are you still mourning Edgar? It literally became one of your famous one-woman shows, your mourning of Edgar. So GW had to wonder—are you still mourning E?

JR: No, I'm not mourning Edgar, that's gone now. There is a sweetness that remains. But I am still angry at Edgar. I will never forgive him for what he did.

GW: That must have been devastating.

JR: Devastating. I had a sixteen-year-old daughter at the time who got the call that her father had committed suicide, and she had to come and tell me. It was a very rough time for our family. But some good jokes have come out of it. I like to say that Edgar committed suicide because we were making love and I took the bag off of my head. I solve everything with humor—he went from the bed to the window.

GW: True or false—Joan Rivers is the only person on this planet who has had more plastic surgery than Michael Jackson.

JR: Absolutely such a lie. I am so tired of this. I came out because I was so sick of sitting there with a room full of women saying to me, "What is it like?" and they are talking through the parts in their hair. I came out just to say to everybody, "Don't believe these people that are saying to you, 'I am naturally beautiful, I'm sixty-five, and I've done nothing.' "

GW: There is still no denying that one of your favorite hobbies is reversing the age process.

JR: Excuse me?!! Absolutely. Look at the ladies I'm with—we are all dipped in formaldehyde.

GW: You say you are sixty-five, but you've been sixty-five for the last ten years, Joan.

JR: Actually it's twelve, but I've watched Sophia Loren get younger than me, Elizabeth Taylor get younger than me. I've watched a whole group of ladies get younger than I am, but I'm the only one who gets picked on.

GW: Who is the phoniest person in Hollywood?

JR: Russell Crowe—phooey. First of all, I hope he never stops to talk to me on the red carpet of an award show, because I don't think he's learned to bathe yet. The man needs a good bar of Joan Rivers Fragrant one hundred percent French Mill soap.

GW: Who is your favorite authoress of all time?

JR: Edith Wharton, hands down, because she *got* it. Because she holds up. You go back and read *The Custom of the Country* anytime, and it's timeless.

GW: Joan, darling, GW sometimes feels that he suffers from tri-polar disorder instead of bipolar disorder. You are the ageless icon of American princesses, so how does Joan Rivers temper her violent mood swings?

JR: And I have them. I scream. I will go into a closet and scream and come out. I really do. Also, I say what I think, and then it's gone. I cannot hold a grudge.

GW: What are the other guidelines that you try to live by?

JR: Don't look back, don't dwell on the past. So your father slept with you! That was forty years ago—tough. Get on with it. And, also don't worry about anybody else—wear blinders. Never forget that, on a bad day, count your blessings, because they could always be worse. If you think you've hit the bottom, there is always the gutter.

GW: Who is the peer that you idol-worship the most? The one that riles the most envy in Joan Rivers?

JR: Robin Williams and Chris Rock—those are the ones where I just go, "Damn, why didn't I think of that?!"

GW: Do you think that you will ever get married again?

JR: Never, absolutely not—but for ten carats, maybe.

GW: Would you agree that you owe a great deal of your career to Johnny Carson?

JR: I owed my career to Johnny Carson in the beginning. And I think that is one of the reasons he was so angry with me, because he in some way felt that he owned me. When I left, he never forgave me.

GW: And he still doesn't speak to you. Who is your all-

time favorite Hollywood director? Please don't say
Steven Spielberg or Chi Chi LaRue.

JR: Robert Altman.

GW: Joan darling, you are still tart, still taut, still very
much a bitch on wheels! We live for Joan Rivers.

JR: Thank God.

{ DEBBIE REYNOLDS }

T here was a time, way back in the day—when the landmark hotel Essex House on Central Park South, New York City—was a fusty, dusty home-away-from-home, long-term residence for the old-school Hollywood legends who often took refuge on the East Coast; think Judy Garland and Debbie Reynolds. This, of course, was way before the Middle East petro-dollars hoovered up, re-configured, and reimagined this hostelry, which today is the Jumeirah Essex House. To this day, every time I saunter down Central Park South past this hotel, I cannot help but think of that afternoon in December of 1996 when Debbie Reynolds herself opened the door to her musty junior suite dressed in a dowdy, threadbare frock, bed-head and all—and a hot iron steaming from her right hand! Golden-age Hollywood had long dubbed her "the girl next door" and she clearly was living up to her myth.

The writer had clearly interrupted her banal and rather personal household chores. But this Hollywood grande dame was totally unfazed, and had not a care in the world about her dotty dishabille. She was so warm and so genuinely effusive and game for our afternoon tête-à-tête. And so after she poured tea, it was truly time to read the tea leaves.

GW: I had assumed that you'd truly retired from the cinema, Debbie Reynolds.

DR: I did. I haven't done feature films in twenty-five years. Instead of me sitting around waiting for an agent to get me work, I put an act together and went to Vegas. I had children to raise. And since I kept having bad marriages . . .

GW: [Starts to laugh.] I don't mean to laugh . . .

DR: That's all right—many people have this problem.

GW: Your daughter, Carrie Fisher, has taken charge of your career and put you back in film.

DR: That is true. Carrie called me in Vegas at around midnight. She said, "Mother, I've had this wonderful idea from Albert Brooks. It's a movie, Mother, and it's possible you can get this part." I accommodated Carrie, so she wouldn't yell at her mother. She loves to boss me around.

GW: Were you nervous reemerging to take on this part?

DR: I was a wreck. I developed ulcers, because I had to learn this enormous part.

GW: You've spent all your money collecting Hollywood

memorabilia for your museum in Las Vegas. Do you really have Dorothy's—

DR: —slippers and the gingham dress? Yes.

GW: Would one be able to find Mae West's vibrators amongst the artifacts?

DR: Well, I know who probably has them. She always surrounded herself with men. So she had this one secretary who is still alive who I think has all her personal items. But I don't think she ever bothered with a vibrator. She used the actual thing twice a day.

GW: Has Debbie Reynolds ever forgiven Elizabeth Taylor for stealing her husband Eddie Fisher?

DR: When Mike Todd and Elizabeth were married, I was her bridesmaid. He died in a plane crash, and she just fell apart. I heard almost when she did, and when I arrived at the house, the press was everywhere. I called Eddie, he flew home, and I sent him right up there. I didn't think it would go anywhere, because he is not her type. And that is exactly what happened, because she threw him out after a year and a half. Of course, it broke up our marriage, and devastated me and my daughter. Our only son was only six months old.

GW: Have you seen E.T. since?

DR: We were on the same boat going to Europe, and I was with my second husband, so I sent her a note saying we should have dinner and talk this out. She came with Richard Burton. We talked about it. I said, "That was really a wrong move, Elizabeth." She said, "Yes, well I hope you forgive me for it, because it was very selfish. I needed somebody, and I didn't really care." But that's thirty-eight years ago. It's done, it's past, but people still ask me about that.

GW: Life goes on, Debbie. Tell me about your next film, *In and Out.*

DR: It's a movie based on the true story of when Tom Hanks won his Oscar for *Philadelphia* and thanked his drama teacher, and mentioned that he was gay, which is something the drama teacher had rarely admitted. Kevin Kline is the drama teacher, and Matt Dillon plays his student who is up for an Oscar, and I play Kevin's mother.

GW: I know you'll be brilliant in it, Debbie. You're still America's sweetheart.

{ CARRIE FISHER }

T alking to the smartest, wittiest people on earth is one of the greatest thrills of my life. And this moment is one I will always cherish forever. I do believe that Carrie Fisher was a better writer than she was a member of the Screen Actors Guild. And yes, indeed she will forever be *Star Wars*' Princess Leia Organa, and too, the first princess of Hollywood nepotism which continues to be a long-standing tradition—just ask Casey Affleck or Paris Jackson. But Carrie Fisher, in fact, was a brilliant writer. Another brilliantly quirky fact to all this is probably that I may be the only writer in history to have interviewed her mother Debbie Reynolds [February 1997], her father Eddie Fisher [not included in this compendium], and Carrie Fisher herself. The outpouring of grief that Christmas of 2016 when Carrie's heart exploded on that first-class flight from Heathrow en route to LAX was too much to bear, most of all for her mother, who we all know, died suddenly the day before Carrie's funeral. Theirs was, indeed, a sad but real Hollywood ending. . . .

GW: You are one of those rare creatures in that concrete jungle called Hollywood. You really have no ene-mies. Everyone—and I mean everyone—loves Carrie Fisher.

CF: Oh, not so fast. I don't know who you've talked to. Certainly there are people who like me, but then there are those who don't know me who gossip about me. You can't believe the things I've heard.

GW: What's one of the most outrageous rumors you've heard about yourself lately?

CF: The most outrageous one of late is that I've slipped on heroin. The one great thing I did, in terms of living out here, is that I never found a heroin dealer.

GW: Well, I am glad you brought up that subject. A friend of yours, a Republican Operative by the name of R. Gregory Stevens, overdosed at your mansion.

CF: This friend of mine had a very dangerous job. He ran presidential elections in very unstable countries, so for him to have died anywhere else was like Patton dying in a car accident. He did drugs. A lot of people were staying at my house, which is why he was sleep-ing with me. He came home around midnight, and he and I got up and talked. He was very tired, and he then went to bed. When I got into bed, I put a pillow between us and I woke him up. We watched TV for a little bit. I was woken up in the morning by my friend Bruce Cohen because we were going to have tango lessons. I had planned to make soufflé that morning. And I went around the bed to wake up Greg and he was dead.

GW: Oh my God!

CF: And from the first moment I blamed myself. I thought I'd put the pillow on his face. I was in shock for months. I thought I had killed him because it had happened on my watch and I had failed to save him. They say his body was so worn out from drug use that if it hadn't happened that night it would've happened on another one.

GW: And you live in this legendary Beverly Hills mansion, built in the 1930s, where Bette Davis lived and where also the famous costume designer Edith Head lived.

CF: Bette Davis lived here. Robert Armstrong built it. He played the filmmaker in *King Kong*.

GW: There must be so many ghosts roaming those grounds.

CF: No . . . no, but we had Greg for a while. I was totally convinced, which kind of made me happy, because I kept thinking, Please don't go.

GW: What do you mean?

CF: Lights would go on and off, and I had this toy machine, that when you touched it it would say, "Fuck you! Eat shit! You're an asshole!" And it would go off in the night, by itself, in my closet. I was a nut for a year, and in that year I took drugs again.

GW: Did you have an exorcist come over and clear the air?

CF: My friends did, and after that things were fine. But you know, he didn't just die in his sleep, he died in mine. So it's still not gone, and I don't think it will ever be.

GW: Well, now you're back at center stage again, as it were, with what is probably your Act Five, this one-woman show.

CF: And I'm singing in it, too, which I haven't done in thirty-three years. It's an unauthorized autobiography.

GW: It's funny, your mother sat for an interview with me in 1997, your father in 1999. I'll never forget going to meet your mother at the Essex House hotel and walking in to the room and she was steaming her clothes over an ironing board.

CF: That must have been a blip. She lives next door to me, to my compound which I call "Kennecuntport."

GW: And speaking of Kennecuntport, I found it very intriguing to know that you had a very cute houseguest.

CF: You mean James Blunt. Yes, he was here for about four months, and he ended up staying in my bathroom a lot because it has a piano in there and the acoustics are good.

GW: And did James Blunt pay the rent? I hear he's cute, sensitive, tall, and pale.

CF: I will never tell and I don't know if I am that sort of landlady.

GW: Oh please! If it was moi, I would be like, "All right James, put down the lyric book and show me some bedroom judo."

CF: Yeah, like on your knees. No, I have a little more class than that. I am a very decent human being when it comes to other people. I don't tell.

GW: Okay, so something happened.

CF: Absolutely not, but I did become his therapist. He was a soldier. This boy has seen awful stuff. Every time James hears fireworks or anything like that, his heart beats faster and he gets "fight or flight." You know, he comes from a long line of soldiers dating back to the tenth century. He would tell me these horrible stories. He was a captain, a reconnaissance soldier. I became James's therapist. So it would have been unethical to sleep with my patient.

GW: I would be remiss if I didn't ask how you ended up in *Star Wars*.

CF: I slept with some nerd. I hope it was George.

GW: You weren't sure?

CF: No . . . I took too many drugs to remember.

GW: And that famous swimsuit from the movie, do you own it?

CF: No, but I will have to borrow it from George sometime when I am really depressed and I want to be even more depressed. I get along very well with George Lucas. He always comes to my birthday party. I also wear the wig from the movie in my show.

GW: Your poor daughter, Billie . . . she is what, like fourteen going on twenty-four?

CF: She's got my mouth and she's got my brains.

GW: She should be best friends with Courtney Love's daughter.

CF: She is. They are friends. Courtney lived next door to us; Frances stayed over the other night.

GW: After an eleven-month marriage to Paul Simon, all he left you with was one of his acoustic guitars.

CF: And nine songs written about me.

GW: And Dan Aykroyd, with whom you got cold feet at the altar.

CF: Yeah, because he would have cheated on me for years and years. But it would have been very funny. And he's adorable and we had a lovely whatever-the-hell-it-was. That was like a rebound from everything else.

GW: And you've hinted that someone you like may move in with you.

CF: And the funny thing is, since someone died here there have been more people living here than ever before. You kind of expect people to say, "So where did it happen?" No one has ever done that.

GW: And what does your Dr. Feelgood have you on these days to keep your bipolar disorder at bay?

CF: Oh, man, name it. I take Tegretol, Seroquel, Lamictal, Topamax.

GW: But no Percocet.

CF: No darling, that's the bad news.

GW: How many pills a day?

CF: About seven.

GW: I guess that's not bad.

CF: Talk to my liver about that.

GW: Is there a day that you can go without taking any pills?

CF: No, I am a mental diabetic.

GW: Well, as you have said in the past, "Instant gratification takes too long."

CF: That's right.

GW: And your new show at the Geffen Playhouse. You and David Geffen are friends, and I know you don't like to talk about other people, but I am asking: Is it true, as the blogs say, that he is dating actor Seann William Scott?

CF: I don't know, but I would doubt it. That's just the same as saying he married Keanu Reeves when they had never even met. I was actually with David at the Geffen when he ran into Keanu. He said to Keanu, "Was it as good for you as it was for me?" They had never even met, and all that stuff had come out about them being married.

GW: Well, count your blessings, Carrie. "The Force" is with you.

Marc
Jacobs

{ MARC JACOBS }

APRIL 1987

I t had been a full week since the auspicious debut of Marc Jacobs for Perry Ellis and the fashion world was agog. The critics had more than given the ponytailed, just-turned-twenty-seven-year-old fashion designer the benefit of the doubt and were now convinced that he was more than willing, and even more capable of leading the multi-million dollar fashion house of Perry Ellis into the 1990s and beyond.

As we all know it didn't really turn out that way. But part of the charm and intrigue for my compendium of interviews here is the simple, fascinating fact that they capture a moment in time and that they are timeless, vintage gems. At the time of this interview *R.O.M.E.* was hailing Marc Jacobs as "the next Calvin Klein" and force of American fashion. Today, through all his trials and tribulations, and his dramatic and roller-coaster personal life—he is still one of the most influential fashion designers in the world.

His office at the showroom/studios of Perry Ellis was chock-full of staff that Tuesday afternoon in 1987 when Marc Jacobs sat for this tête-à-tête with George Wayne. The designer was behind his desk standing, and tugging on the perennial Marlboro Light cigarette and dressed as if he were at some Hamptons summer bungalow in a faded Stephen Sprouse sweatshirt, Levi jeans, and his then-signature square-toed motorcycle boots.

All eyes were on the video monitor. Marc and a sprinkling of his associates were reviewing one of the many post-show interviews, the post-mortem, as it were, after that April 10, 1987, fashion show. The interview in question was being conducted by the most revered and influential television fashionista in history—the one and only—Elsa Klensch of the Cable News Network (CNN). "No one can fully step into someone else's shoes," the American enfant terrible of fashion was quipping to diva Elsa. "I can only do my best." That has long been his principal foil since daring to take over the house of Perry Ellis just a few months previous. He had, since then, been constantly tamping down expectations about his new job and what he planned to do to revive this moribund, blue-chip American fashion brand.

But the mavens loved the show that April, and that had to have given the young designer a boost of confidence, not only to him, but his entire team. "Major!!" was the spin from the *Vogue* creative director, André Leon Talley. "Fabulous!" was the declarative of another fashion-critic legend, Polly Allen Mellen of *Allure*. "Exuberant!" was how Frank DeCaro of New York *Newsday* summed it up. "Marc is one of our most exciting new talents," offered the well-noted fashion fore-caster Bernie Ozer.

Marc Jacobs was very much aware at the time that he could not afford to be mediocre. The expectations were that high. When all was said and done, he was just another young, brash designer backed by the Japanese financiers of Kashiyama, who would have no problem pulling the rug out from under him, if he could not deliver. Time was very much of the essence. It was a catch-22 to say the very least. But he delivered on that debut for Perry Ellis at the Puck Building on Lafayette Street—and without question had catapulted his own personal celebrity to brand-new heights. He has certainly come a long way since selling clothes at Charivari—that's for sure!

GW: Did you go to any other shows during Fashion Week?

MJ: I went to [Ronaldus] Shamask. I really enjoyed it. I thought it was really good. I wanted to go to Isaac's [Mizrahi] show, but I had work to do here and I couldn't get out. And Friday morning I had to do an interview with CBS and I really wanted to go to Mr. Beene's show because I go every single season, and I didn't get to go so I was very upset about that. It's really nice to go to other people's shows because, you know, we all get excited by fashion, otherwise we wouldn't be doing it.

GW: So were you happy with the reaction to your show? Most people seem to believe that you did well for yourself, but that Isaac [Mizrahi] stole your thunder this season.

MJ: People can think whatever they want. I don't sit around and think to myself, "God, I created the most incredible thing," or anything like that. I just do what I do and if people like it, or they don't like it, there is not much more one can do than that. This whole notion of people feeling that one collection is better, or that one collection is good or isn't, doesn't bother me. I mean, there are good things in every collection just as how there are bad things. I certainly am not going to drive myself crazy over any of that kind of stuff. I think that Isaac is an extraordinary talent. But nobody wears only one designer.

GW: You must feel like the weight of the world is off your shoulders?

MJ: A little bit. But there is no way I could live up to everyone's expectations after this first show. Because the pressure was so great, and it was created by people who just wanted this to be the most amazing thing we've ever seen. We are all too jaded, and we have all seen too much. And there really isn't anything new under the sun. You just do what you think is right.

GW: Do you feel like you're on firm ground here at Perry Ellis? After all, Patricia Pastor also had a contract and she was fired.

MJ: Well, nothing is ever carved in stone you know, but I think the people here are happy with what I've done. And you know, only the future will tell what happens or what doesn't happen, and that is fine . . .

GW: You can live with anything, you go with the flow.

MJ: Well, what can you do? If I sit down all the time worrying, Am I going to be here? Am I not going to be here? I'll never get anything done at all.

GW: What is going to determine the success of this collection?

MJ: Well, I think in terms of creating or bringing back the energy to this company, because we are already very successful. Sales have been really good. It's always a different story when you go to shows then see the clothes on the rack. A few of the mavens had a problem with the presentation because some thought it was too outrageous, too Downtown, or whatever. But it's hard sometimes for these people to see through and to see what the clothes are all about. I basically told those girls to do what they wanted to do, because I hired them because of who they were, not because of what I could make them into. I'm sure that a lot of people would've been happier to see a very staged, very simple, quiet presentation. But sales have been good. I mean, we have really good clothes downstairs, and the reaction has been basically very good.

GW: Your coming to Perry Ellis was like the biggest shock of all! I mean, I remember the night before the announcement, we were dancing the night away at El Morocco! And the next morning I woke up and opened the *New York Times* to read you were going to head the house of Ellis. Did you not tell a soul?

MJ: No, I didn't tell anyone.

GW: Not one word?

MJ: Not one word.

GW: How did this all happen? Did you approach them? Did they approach you?

MJ: No, they approached me, and it was all very casual at first. They asked if I would be interested and I said yes. And then we sat down and talked about it and they asked how I would define Perry Ellis. And I really remember my feelings about Perry Ellis when I was a student and how amazing I thought this company was because of the spirit and energy that came out of this place. I said my whole image of Perry Ellis was really classic American sportswear, but there was also something there that made it so much more special.

GW: So this wasn't a long, delicate negotiation?

MJ: No. It all happened very quickly. It was over in a couple of days.

GW: You must be getting paid a lot of money. Do you have equity in Perry Ellis and all that?

MJ: No. I mean, I have a nice offer, but it's not like I sold my apartment and moved into a Fifth Avenue townhouse and bought a country home and a yacht. I'm really pretty simple when it comes to that stuff.

GW: But how could you not regret giving up your name?

MJ: I don't regret it at all. More people really know that I am here behind this collection than when I was just Marc Jacobs doing the Marc Jacobs label. In terms of my ego, it's no big deal at all. And now I'm having the opportunity to do so many things which in the end makes it that much more rewarding. All the other stuff that comes with this job is really more rewarding for me as a person than anything I could have gotten just having my name on a label.

GW: Did you play with dolls as a child?

MJ: No.

GW: Has it been a lifelong desire to design clothes?

MJ: Yeah . . . I would say since I was about thirteen or fourteen. I was always customizing clothes, and when I was thirteen or fourteen, I decided that I wanted to be involved in fashion.

GW: What kind of student were you at Parsons? Did you coast, or were you always studying?

MJ: No. I worked very hard and I was working at Charivari after school and on the weekends selling clothes. I really wanted to be around designer clothes and it also gave me a very interesting education in terms of, I suppose, the designer mentality of the customer in New York.

GW: I understand that your startling photos in *Vanity Fair* provoked a violent reaction from America's heartland. That the *V.F.* offices were flooded. How do you feel about that?

MJ: Really? I had no idea! It really wasn't thought out or calculated at all. There were a lot of ideas and a lot of things we talked about doing. And I have so much trust in Stephen Meisel that I didn't feel I had to worry about it at all. Basically what that photo said to me was that I was like a free spirit and I was out there.

{ DAVID COPPERFIELD }

FEBRUARY 1996 & NOVEMBER 2012

L as Vegas is the American frontier for the grand spec-
tacle! And as such there is no other place on earth
where the world's grand master of illusion would
find his oasis than in the desert of Nevada. Since
the age of twelve as a boy growing up in Metuchen, New Jersey, and already a practiced magician, David Copperfield knew
all along that his professional calling was destined to end up in
this land of gilt and illusion. He remains to this day our version
of Houdini and the ultimate definition of a "zillionaire"—as
in rich, rich, rich! Have you ever been to his own private island
in the Bahamas archipelago known as Musha Cay? Of course
not! That right has to be by invitation only.

When I did this interview with the master magician, he
was the envy of men half his age all over the globe because of
his years-long engagement to the German supermodel Claudia
Schiffer. Yet, GW was immediately won over by how humble

and relatable he was despite acquiring all the assets and trappings that come with living the über-American dream. . . . He and Mark Wahlberg are the only two personalities that I have ever interviewed twice for my column in *Vanity Fair*.

GW: A lot of people fail to understand what Claudia Schiffer saw in you. I guess you must be hung like Rasputin.

DC: It's true.

GW: Your magic amazes the world—from the American to the Zulu.

DC: It's funny: when I go to third-world countries, people actually believe it's not illusion. I spend a lot of time convincing people—for example, in Indonesia, Malaysia, even some parts of Europe—that what I do is illusion. I work as hard to make my art form respected as entertainment form—like music and dance and drama or cinema.

GW: And how did you find this calling?

DC: Like everybody, we all search to find what makes us acceptable with our peer group when we are kids. What was it for you?

GW: Being on the quiz team.

DC: Is that right? And you excelled at it and all the kids at school thought you were cool. For me, when I did magic, I got the same kind of feeling.

GW: And when did David Kotkin from Metuchen, New Jersey, reinvent himself as David Copperfield?

DC: I'm constantly reinventing myself. I'm constantly changing. I've been on TV for eighteen years now.

I'm thirty-nine, and I keep changing the face of magic and myself all the time.

GW: All right, now that we've done that BS, let's get back to you and the Fräulein supermodel. . . .

DC: And Rasputin . . .

GW: You get to sleep with Claudia Schiffer on a regular basis, and that makes you one of the most envied men in the world. Expound on that first meeting for the umpteenth time.

DC: Well, she came to see my show in Berlin, Germany, two years ago. So I brought her up onstage, and I read her mind, and she read mine. And then I took her in my arms, and I flew with her. And I think that's a pretty darn good date. And then we sat and talked all night. And we haven't stopped talking since.

GW: On what date did you start having sex?

DC: This is where you put "long pause." When I was fourteen years old, I started having sex.

GW: On what date did you start having sex with her?

DC: I can't tell that. I have to protect her dignity and her womanhood.

GW: How often do you see each other?

DC: We have a two-week rule. We're never apart for more than two weeks.

GW: By the way, where do you buy your bronzer? And what kind do you use?

DC: I don't. You can rub.

GW: [GW pulls a finger across DC's forehead] It's natural pigment!

DC: It's the sun.

GW: Tanning salons?

DC: Absolutely not.

GW: What is your next grand illusion?

DC: An indoor tornado, which will be the most amazing thing you have ever seen.

GW: I think the meanest thing I've ever read about you was from some hack in London, of course, who questioned your integrity by writing that you are "an egomaniac, a control freak, a closet homosexual with a fake relationship and an even faker tan." How do you deal with stuff like that?

DC: Except for the last two, it's all true.

GW: So you are a closet homosexual!

DC: Be careful, young man—the last three. I think people are always going to have their own agenda. The more you are in the public eye, the more the people are going to try to pick you apart.

GW: Hy and Rebecca, your parents, must be proud of you.

DC: They're great. They're really, really great. I think I'm living my father's dream. So it's nice to watch it through his eyes.

2012

GW: Talk to me about the eleven islands in the Bahamian archipelago that you own. Naomi Campbell has been there, Oprah has been there, and the Google guy

Sergey Brin got married on one of your Bahama islands!

DC: Yeah, and so did Penelope Cruz and Javier Bardem.

GW: Not to mention the incredible four-story bachelor pad on Fifty-seventh Street in Manhattan that you never use.

DC: My fiancée, Chloe Gosselin, is there all the time with our two-year-old daughter, Sky.

GW: Sky certainly has a palace in the sky. Thank you, David.

Philip Johnson

Laura Baran

{ PHILIP JOHNSON }

NOVEMBER 1998

P hilip Cortelyou Johnson was ninety-two years old that day in September 1998 when he strode to greet me from his office in the iconic Seagram Building which he helped Ludwig Mies van der Rohe design. He shook my hand firmly and smiled broadly saying how excited he was to be part of the November issue of *Vanity Fair*. The iconic architect was still a quasi–press whore after all these years, and I found that highly amusing.

He was in a dark pink pinstripe suit, so elegant, so distinguished, and still a fit sprite, now well into his nineties, as he gave a guided tour of his offices and the beautiful view they offered off Park Avenue. Fifteen minutes later we sat to speak, and as I reminisce I realize I was probably a bit thrown by his assured air and his signature big, round, black glasses. I mean this was a lion of Manhattan's upper echelons of high society.

A supposed "BFF" of Jackie O. [Onassis] and at his age still a valued curator, too, for the Museum of Modern Art.

GW: GW regards this audience with the legend that is Philip Johnson as a historic moment. But please, sir, we need to know: Is Viagra really the miracle drug many claim it is?

PJ: I don't know. At ninety-two . . . you don't ask questions like that.

GW: Well, are you still popping Prozac?

PJ: No. I gave up Prozac. I don't take any pills.

GW: Would you agree that Philip Johnson is the architect most responsible for defining twentieth-century American architecture?

PJ: No. What I am responsible for is pointing to some kids that I liked very much. They're almost reaching seventy now, but they are my kids. The best known are Peter Eisenman and Frank Gehry.

GW: Well, you've never been shy about making proclamations.

PJ: I speak in proclamations!

GW: GW must be one of the few who hate Philip Johnson's Sony Building. If that's what postmodernism is about, you can keep it, honey! It's like a dowdy dowager with botched plastic surgery.

PJ: Good for you. I like the building, but it doesn't come into my main oeuvre.

GW: What is Philip Johnson working on now?

PJ: The gay and lesbian cathedral in Dallas. We're working on that very hard—the Cathedral of Hope.

GW: It's sort of amazing that at this point in your life you choose to do something so controversial.

PJ: Well, they asked me. And they liked my cathedral in L.A. I said no. But then I said, Why not? I'd work for the devil himself if he were interested in architecture.

GW: Was Jackie O. one of your best friends?

PJ: No. I used to see her out at parties. I didn't know her well. That was a media creation.

GW: GW had the impression that you were on the telephone with Jackie O. every night.

PJ: Oh, no—she and I made an appearance to save Grand Central Station, and were budsy-wudsy for ten minutes.

GW: Tell GW about those vodka parties at your Glass House, with Andy Warhol passed out in the corner and Truman Capote reeking from vodka breath.

PJ: Andy came out once. Truman never sloshed vodka in my house.

GW: Okay, then we must discuss your *Titanic*.

PJ: My what?

GW: Your *Titanic*—1932, and your days of embracing Hitler.

PJ: Oh, heavens. A minor period in my life.

GW: Was it that minor?

PJ: Yes, it was. I was taking a vacation.

GW: You actually saw Adolf Hitler in the flesh?

PJ: I went to a rally once. I hardly understood German

at the time, but he was hypnotizing. But it was also very, very stupid. [It was] the greatest misjudgment of my life. I regretted it right away, and it's haunted me ever since. I was old enough to know better. I have no excuses at all—just terrible regret.

GW: I've read that you had a nervous breakdown at Harvard in the twenties.

PJ: I was out three or four years.

GW: And was that a result of your not being able to acknowledge that you were gay?

PJ: That's right. In the twenties it was terrible.

GW: Are you still married?

PJ: I'm not married.

GW: But you have a significant other—your "husband," David Whitney.

PJ: We came together in 1960. Haven't you got a significant other?

GW: No.

PJ: Playing the field, huh?

GW: I should, but nobody seems to want me. Don't you think I'm a great catch?

PJ: It's called luck. You have lots of time, so play the field.

{ BRIDGET HALL }

Bridget Hall was very much part and parcel of the golden age of the supermodel as ingénue.

Before even the arrival of Kate Moss, this all-American girl from Texas defined the era and the aura of 1990s supermodel-dom. To this day, she remains one of the coolest, realest, most down-to-earth gals that I ever have met! We spent many a night bonding and becoming bosom buddies and drinking partners at the haute-boîte that defined New York City at the time—and that was impresario Roy Liebenthal's legendary Café Tabac in Manhattan's East Village.

"B," as all who grew to adore her fondly called her, spent her days minting coins as the five-star supermodel and her nights knocking back Heineken beers and owning the pool-room of Café Tabac, which was then the hottest of hot spots in Gotham City. Every night was an incredible night at Café

Tabac. What Café Tabac was in the nineties is what my favorite boîte, Omar's La Ranita, is to the twenty-first-century Manhattan demimonde: that one restaurant, bar, and incredibly special salon. I will always remember that night B dropped a bombshell while we were shooting billiards in the cool poolroom of Café Tabac.

Christy Turlington was at the main bar throwing back shots with Bono Vox—yes, that Bono! And Bridget and GW were getting equally wasted and gossiping the night away. It was on that night when she revealed to me that she lost her virginity to a very, very famous A-list Hollywood box-office superstar—and still to this day a serial modelizer. You can well imagine that I gasped and spewed my "GW Mimsy" across the room. For those who don't know the George Wayne cocktail of choice—the GW Mimsy is a concoction of the finest cuvée served over ice in a "piscine" (red wine goblet preferably) with a "spooge" of premium vodka and fresh, squeezed blood-orange juice. It is my drink of choice and of course, as always, on that particular night it put GW in the perfect mood to probe and parry.

"Lord have mercy, B!!" I remember squealing. "Are you telling me that HE was the one who popped your Texas cherry?" She admitted again that that was indeed the facts of life. And you wonder why to this day the notorious Lothario and legendary A-list actor remains hooked on supermodels.

Suffice it to say, that this is one of GW's all-time memorable interviews—most so because it was with a near and dear friend and one of my all-time favorite girls in the world.

GW: So give me the juicy on that story I heard about Jack Nicholson chasing you around the pool of the Chateau Marmont.

BH: It's true, but it wasn't that bad.

GW: So his tongue wasn't hanging out of his mouth?

BH: No. He said, "Hi, nice to see you again." I said, "What do you mean to see me again? It's my first time meeting you." But he seems very nice.

GW: So he wasn't a dirty old man?

BH: He probably was, but I left.

GW: Your life is like a fairy tale. Here you are, a high-school dropout, poor white trash from Texas, now the emerging supermodel of the millennium. And all of seventeen years old!

BH: It's not really a fairy tale. It's a lot harder than it seems. Sometimes I wish I didn't drop out of school.

GW: Tell me about your childhood.

BH: My childhood was cool. It was all right. I was always the tallest, skinniest kid in school, tomboy.

GW: Were you the ugly duckling?

BH: In a way I was. I had friends who would always put me down. They would call me "Chicken Legs." I would feel hurt.

GW: Tell me about the worst day ever on the set of a fashion shoot?

BH: The worst day is any day I have to get up really early, with a photographer who shoots really slow. And keeps me really late at night.

GW: Do you realize that not since the trinity—Naomi, Linda, and Christy—has there been a super, super girl to emerge like you?

BH: I guess that's great. But I am trying to get into acting.

GW: I know for a fact that you've had a few boy problems. Things didn't work out with you and Leonardo DiCaprio. For a while you were chasing Stephen Dwarf—excuse me, Stephen Dorff. And he had the nerve to treat you like doo-doo.

BH: I don't know what I want right now. They were very nice guys, but prettier in pictures.

GW: Who is the bitchiest supermodel you've ever met in your life?

BH: There's plenty of 'em . . . and no names!

GW: Come on, B, you've got to give me some names.

BH: No names . . .

GW: There are so many bitchy supermodels, and you can't give me one name? Let me hazard a guess: Linda?

BH: No names. Linda's been nice to me.

GW: All right—light another cigarette, honey, get another Heineken, and get ready.

BH: I'm ordering it up, another Heineken . . .

GW: I know that's your favorite beverage. And I know that you've lost your cherrystone, but I want to know to whom.

BH: No, not saying. I'm not gonna say that.

GW: When did you lose it?

BH: When I was fifteen.

GW: Was it to a little farm boy in the trailer park?

BH: No, I'm not saying, George.

GW: Where?

BH: My mom's gonna read this!

GW: Honey, your mother must know you are a growing woman!

BH: Okay, in a hotel room in New York.

GW: Okay, now I want to know the man who took your chastity!

BH: It's going to take about twelve Heinekens to get that answer.

GW: What do you do in your spare time, when you are not forced to be fabulous for the camera?

BH: I sleep and try to get over my hangover, watch MTV.

GW: Not since the seventies has the name Hall been such a force in fashion. I can't believe some queenious fashion editor hasn't been inspired to pair Bridget Hall and Jerry Hall in a shoot together.

BH: I think she is pretty cool. I would love to be in a shoot with Jerry Hall. It would show that Texans are ruling!

{ MILTON BERLE }

A fter this interview hit the newsstand for *Vanity Fair*, I got a phone call from a close college friend who was back home in Savannah, Georgia. Even after all those years, he clearly had not lost the opportunity to show how much smarter and culturally astute he was than I was.

"Why didn't you ask 'Uncle Miltie' about his enormous cock?" he postured. "You know he is supposed to have one of the biggest cocks in Hollywood."

I had not been aware of this Hollywood lore. And looking back, my perennial reasoning was that GW was still, in 1994, an ingénue to documenting the ins and outs of Hollywood Babylon. The size and girth of Milton Berle's phallus was then news to me. And even had I known I probably would not have broached the subject to this iconic curmudgeon. I was still a shy, young arbiter learning the ropes—and giddy with the great fortune of having his own column in the most prestigious magazine of celebrity culture in the world. So, despite my seemingly endless phallus mania, that particular subject with this particular subject was never broached.

That said, it is more important to note that Hollywood no longer conjures true professionals, true masters of the acting/comedic craft like the endless legend that will always be Milton Berle. And he was certainly in fine form the day we did this GW Q&A. I was most fascinated about what he had to say about RuPaul Charles, the drag queen impresario who my college friend and I had known from our formative years spent in Athens, Georgia, which was then the nexus of cool-college-town-counterculture. And where we both first met and were mesmerized by the likes of RuPaul and Lady Bunny doing drag shows at the famous 40 Watt Club in downtown Athens, GA.

And I can tell you that even back then RuPaul was one smart, clever, very ambitious, and very calculating queen. And if "Uncle Miltie" were still around today, there is no doubt he would agree. . . .

GW: So tell me, Mr. Berle, what was the problem between you and RuPaul at the MTV music awards?

MB: Well, MTV asked me if I would make an appearance, teaming me up with . . . what's his name? Rude-Paul? Because in the forties and fifties I wore dresses in shtick and doing bits. So person . . . what's his name?

GW: RuPaul.

MB: Rude-Paul, this female impersonator—I don't know

how long he's been in show business, maybe two months. So they figured me being of my era it would be a good comedic point if we both came out together wearing drag. I am one that respects what I'm doing, and the word is rehearse, practice, know your lines. When he finally showed, he said, "Don't worry about me, I know exactly what I'm doing," in a very gay-ish way. So the first time I met him was when we walked on. My line was "I used to wear dresses, but I don't anymore." And he was supposed to say, "Why don't you?" And my answer was "Because it's a drag." But instead he said, "What do you wear, diapers?" Being a reference in my mind that I'm a little over-aged; that I possibly pee in my pants. I was ready to hit him with a left hook to the stomach, right on camera.

GW: You were the first real TV star, Mr. Television! You made your movie debut with Charlie Chaplin! What more could Uncle Miltie want from life?

MB: Nothing more. I was brought up in show business. I was the Buster Brown boy when I was five, in 1913!

GW: What's the greatest honor you've ever received?

MB: Well, I was the first comedian-actor to appear simultaneously on the cover of *Time* and *Newsweek*. I was also the first one inducted to the TV Academy Hall of Fame, along with the beloved and terribly missed Lucille Ball.

GW: I hear the secret to your longevity is that you drink a gallon of water every day.

MB: It flushes me . . .

GW: You're a big deal in the Friars Club. What did you think of the Ted Danson–Whoopi Goldberg debacle?

MB: I'm the Abbot Emeritus of the Friars Club. I must take a stand on the Friars Club. I must take a stand on the Friars' behalf. It's no one's business what we do at the club. We only roast people we like, and it's all in jest. It was Whoopi's idea—she wrote the material, she thought it would be funny. It is none of the media's business. This is our own fun, Friars' fun. This was not for public consumption.

GW: What do you think of Roseanne Arnold?

MB: I like her. She has a character going for her and she sticks to her character.

GW: Who do you think are the greatest comedians?

MB: Jack Benny was one of the greatest comedians who ever lived because he was not afraid of pausing, he was not afraid of silence. He took the time, and his timing was the greatest in the world. Woody Allen is one of the giants, and then of the new group, Robin Williams.

GW: Do you still watch television?

MB: I do not watch sitcoms, because they are all the same, the premise. I'm too show-wise.

GW: How is your sex life?

MB: In what respect?

GW: Do you still have orgasms?

MB: What kind of a question is that? Do you wanna test

me? You sound like Howard Stern! I'm not even gonna answer you.

GW: How about the mythic figures you've met? What are some of Uncle Miltie's lasting impressions?

MB: Well, I was in Washington the other day, and I got such a mist in my eyes when I realized that I was at the White House in 1920 and I met Woodrow Wilson.

Barry
White

{ BARRY WHITE }

Without question the opportunity to interview the great Barry White to this day remains one of the highlights of, yes, my rather stellar career! And on that day in September of 1999 when we first spoke, I could hardly contain how intrigued and mesmerized I was by that inimitable distinct velvet baritone. His voice was so seductive even in conversation that throughout the entire interview all I kept thinking to myself was "Gee . . . I am really talking to the sultan of soul!" He had just published his memoir, *Love Unlimited*, when he sat to give this personal serenade to yours truly. And when all was said and done I quickly realized that he was very much aware of the genius he blessed and left this world with.

GW: Barry White is getting ready to go on tour with Earth, Wind and Fire.

BW: Way into the year 2000.

GW: The New Year's Eve Concert with Barry White and Earth, Wind and Fire will be the ticket. Barry White— "Icon of Love." He's been a part of showbiz for forty years.

BW: That's right.

GW: How does he maintain that savoir faire, that legendary growl?

BW: I just keep myself, my thoughts in shape. . . .

GW: Is it a lot of hot tea, lemon juice? No ritual for the throat?

BW: No, no, no ritual for the throat. I don't drink tea or lemon juice.

GW: That's amazing, just a God-given talent.

BW: That's right.

GW: The voice of Barry White can bring a woman to ovulation. Why do you think that is?

BW: I have no idea. I've heard that.

GW: Where was Barry White born?

BW: Galveston, Texas, and raised in Los Angeles.

GW: Your mother was an actress on the MGM studio lot. Around what year was this?

BW: Nineteen fifty-one. She stopped working at MGM when she got pregnant with me. She never went back to acting, or to Hollywood after that. She didn't want to. She wanted to raise and take care of her son.

GW: Come to think of it, at the age of fifteen you were in jail. Was it a murder rap?

BW: No, for burglary.

GW: So you weren't on death row?

BW: [Laughs loudly] No, no. My childhood was super poor. The ghetto of Los Angeles is just as low as the ghetto of Harlem. My family had no money; we had a very meek life. But I fell in love with music, by my mother playing the piano. And one day I came home, when I was five years old. And she lit my soul up, by playing that piano. She would play the "Moonlight" Sonata and all those classical pieces. She could play the hell out of 'em. And that was what fired me up, for playing the piano.

GW: Now you're writing a book.

BW: Yes, I am. People have been asking me for years to write a book about my life. This is the time when I have decided to do it.

GW: "I've made $200 million dollars in five years," you once bragged to the *New York Times*. I hope you have saved some of it.

BW: I still have a lot of it. Believe me.

GW: Barry White has this Midas-like persona. He loves gold, loves wearing it. Down to the brand of cigarette he smokes—Benson and Hedges Gold.

BW: Benson and Hedges Ultra Light Menthol.

GW: Does Barry White growl with disdain when people call him the "sultan of the bedroom"?

BW: Well, to me that's nothing more than a compliment.

GW: You would have to take it as a compliment. How else can you explain your eight children. Is Barry White now in a stable relationship?

BW: Yes. I have a girlfriend going on six years now.

GW: One thing that one can always say is that the one mistress of Barry White will always be his music.

BW: Music, that's one thing you can die with.

GW: Do you ever chant "God Bless America"?

BW: No.

GW: Who do you give thanks to?

BW: I give thanks to myself. I thank me for being dedicated to music, for being loyal to music, for being consistent in music. I thank me for those things.

{ DOLPH LUNDGREN }

O ne of my most captivating early memories of becoming a New Yorker was the first time I finally
gained entry into the hottest, most exclusive
nightclub at the time in 1985 known as Area. I
will never forget that night this wide-eyed arriviste finally
made it past the velvet ropes of that incredible disco in Tribeca
and stood agog at the balustrade, when I quickly realized that
right across the crowded dance floor and thumping music
stood Andy Warhol in deep conversation with Jean-Michel
Basquiat and Tina Chow. GW was starry-eyed beyond belief!
And then suddenly there was even more commotion as Grace
Jones arrived with her Scandinavian mastodon and lover
Dolph Lundgren.

Years later after I became friends with Dolph, I recalled
that moment in my early life as a Manhattan gadabout. We
were having tea in a midtown hotel where he asked me to

meet with him to consider the possibility of ghostwriting a fitness book he was interested in doing. I stupidly turned down the offer, and remember naively telling him that before I write anyone else's book, I would first have to write mine. Of all the great, unforgettable stardust showbiz couples through the decades, Grace and Dolph will forever stand the test of time as one of the most fascinating and fabulous.

In early 1995 we met again for this formal interview, and he was just as charming, just as erudite, and just as gorgeous as the first time I ever set eyes on him. He is not only a karate champion and movie star, but also a former Fulbright scholar, bouncer, and boyfriend of Grace Jones. He is in sum, just one incredible human being. He was in the midst of reviving his film career when we sat to speak.

GW: So, Dolph, darling, tell me about this new movie, *Johnny Mnemonic.*

DL: It's based on a William Gibson story—you know the guy who started the cyberpunk movement? I play a preacher.

GW: So you have a good-guy role?

DL: No, he's a villain, but an interesting villain.

GW: The thing I really dig about you, Dolph, is that you not only have the brawn but the brain. I hear you were a Fulbright scholar!

DL: Yes, that's why I came over here, to go to grad school at MIT.

GW: But weren't you a nightclub bouncer?

DL: I worked at Private Eyes as a doorman, and did a little modeling after I dropped out of school, but I didn't do too well, because they thought I was too big.

GW: Let's go over your relationship with Grace Jones. How did you ever hook up with a wacko like Grace?

DL: She's not a wacko. I'd say she is an eccentric artist. We met backstage at one of her concerts, where I was doing security, as usual.

GW: I used to think that Grace and Dolph were so fabulous! I'll never forget that night at Area when you and Grace made an entrance. You were wearing nothing but a pair of tight leather pants!

DL: Oh God, those were my crazy days!

GW: Another favorite image is that Albert Watson photo— you're both nude, and she's wrapped around you like the only black panther.

DL: I remember that one. It was after I ran into Andy Warhol at a club, and I didn't know who he was, and he came up to me and said, "So what are you famous for?" And I said, "Nothing, as far as I know." And then he did this article on Grace and me in *Interview*.

GW: What did your parents think about Grace?

DL: My mother was very cool, but I think my dad had a few problems. He couldn't figure out what he did wrong, but he came around. Now I've married a Swedish girl.

GW: Yeah, tell me about this plain-Jane you just got married to.

DL: She's not a plain-Jane, no way! She was a fashion stylist and jewelry designer, so we had some similar interests, and of course, she is Swedish.

GW: What do you think about Jean-Claude Van Damme?

DL: Well . . . he's amazingly successful.

GW: Aren't you surprised? He's shot up there, and you are still down here.

DL: No. I moved here because I wanted to be an actor. I was a movie star before having the chance to become an actor, so now I'm trying to backtrack.

GW: Do you think that Hollywood thinks you're a has-been?

DL: Maybe, because in Hollywood they are either at your throat or at your feet. It's the name of the game; it's nothing personal. It's a very cynical business, but I'd like to try and do it a little more on my own terms.

GW: Are there any nude photos of Dolph floating around?

DL: Aaahm . . . no.

GW: Oh come on! You've never posed nude?

DL: I've never seen them. I've never done frontal nudity, but I did a photo with Skrebneski . . .

GW: Frontal?

DL: No, sorry.

GW: Remember that time when I groped you backstage at a concert? This was donkey years ago!

DL: You did? Oh shit! I don't know, maybe I'd had too many drinks.

GW: You didn't seem to mind.

DL: Yeah?

GW: Which of his assets is Dolph the most proud of?

DL: That's a good question. I'm trying to be kinder to my-self, to look more positively. Let's see . . . persistence. If I want to get somewhere, I get there.

{ DENNIS BASSO }

MAY 2004

Y ou all ought to know by now that GW marches to the beat of his own drum. And I would like to believe that trait is shared, too, with the indomitable Dennis Basso. When fashion-folk snobs tried to marginalize his genius as a mere furrier to a few famous stars, he dug deep and stuck to his ultimate ambition, which was to be a recognized and revered and influential American designer of fashion. Now, twelve years after this initial interview, Dennis Basso is a bona fide American fashion star.

With his signature basso profundo (a voice to rival that of Harvey Fierstein) and wit and charm and unmatched generosity to match his ample girth—GW certainly regards DB as a friend and an inspiration. This interview was conducted at his eponymous boutique on Madison Avenue in New York City. It was the most fun and refreshing way to spend an afternoon. As the interview was over and I made my way to stroll down the street to the nearest subway, the designer stopped me in my tracks and insisted that I not leave without one of his latest designer accessories. "These just came in, and you are not leaving here without one," he insisted. I demurred, but Dennis Basso would have none of it. And so shockingly shameless as it would seem, I peered into the rather large gift-wrapped shopping bag, pondering what the hell this could be. As it turned out, it was a rather large tote bag made of the finest mink. I initially refused, and yes, ultimately accepted his gift.

As it turned out, that Dennis Basso mink tote was the perfect fashion accessory a mere two days later as yours truly swished on to an Aeroflot flight and a first-class seat bound for Moscow, Russia, and their 2004 Moscow Fashion Week. I always tell Dennis, seeing each other on the town over the following years, that I regard that wonderful gift as my lucky charm. "It brought me luck in Moscow," I would always tell him, "and the best sex I have ever had in my life!"

I have always been fascinated by Russia, ever since my first visit in 1993. GW was flown to Russia, after the wall of communism crumbled, alongside the likes of Martha Stewart, Fern Mallis, André Balazs, and a few other influential New Yorkers to celebrate the opening of the first Western-styled nightclub in Moscow. That was an unforgettable trip. So of course I was very excited to be visiting Russia again all those many years later. I packed my Prada luggage for what was to be a visit from April 2 to April 11, 2004, for the Moscow Fashion Week at the Tsereteli Art Gallery in that city where sixty designers from Russia, Belarus, and Ukraine were staging their collections. I ended up staying in Moscow for three months, even rented an apartment. I met and ended up having the most incredible love affair with a famous Russian sports superstar with whom I had the most amazing sex, and which to this day I have not been able to equal with any other being on this planet. And that fur bag was the reason we met in the first place.

Most of you may have heard of the legendary Russian figure of lore, Rasputin, the man history refers to as Russia's greatest love machine. Looking back, I would like to think that I was "Rastaputin"—the Jamaican version. The sex with this gorgeous Russian jock blessed with the most gorgeous pink cock was so special that I rented an apartment from this local babushka who happened to be a longtime pianist for the Bolshoi Ballet and who lived steps away from the Kremlin. I would spend my days at Condé Nast on Bolshaya Dmitrovka and in further discovering this amazing city, from the Old Arbat to my favorite Moscow street, the Pereulok Sivtsev Vrazhek, and then going out every night to the chicest, most fabulous clubs and restaurants, gorging on caviar and the purest Russian vodka, and window-shopping along the Stoleshnikov lined with Burberry, Vuitton, Hermès, and Jimmy Choo. And then waking up most mornings next to this stunning Russian jock and glancing out the window to see the famous Kremlin, a ruble's throw away from my rented apartment on Gazetny Lane.

It is still to this day the most amazing three months I have ever spent anywhere in the world! Suffice it to say that I spent enough time in Moscow to be versed in Kremlinology and the ways of the *siloviki* [officials from the Russian military and security forces]. And with the way the despot Vladimir Putin has been acting these days, I am very happy that I experienced that moment then and not now.

I doubt the Moscow of 2017 is a city I truly feel the need to visit or would feel free in. So my memory of it will be forever intertwined with this interview. Elizabeth Taylor, one of the many famous and iconic clients of Dennis Basso, always used to say that white diamonds brought her luck. I always like to tell my friends that it was that Dennis Basso mink tote that brought me the best sex I have ever had in my life!

GW: Rumor has it that you are going to be Liza's next husband—which would be absolutely queenious!

DB: I don't know if I'm going to be Liza's next husband. I think she already has something lined up. But her separation will bring us a little closer together. She is a wonderful girl, very intelligent, and a fabulous entertainer. And I am very happy that she is a part of my life.

GW: I don't know if you or Harvey Fierstein has more of that "gravel" to your voice. Is it naturally unnatural? Or is it a result of the constant stretching of your vocal cords?

DB: I've always had this voice. It is just as much a part of me as the way I walk, my mannerisms, my style. This is really my voice. Maybe it is because I talk a lot, and I like to give a lot of opinions, but I have always had this deep voice.

GW: Where in the Jersey boondocks were you born, Dennis Basso?

DB: I grew up in Morris County, somewhat of a privileged child. I was an only child, a little spoiled, but well mannered. I had the most wonderful, incredible mother, and to this day I think of my parents every single day. They were just great to me, and I think part of who I am today, and the success that I have been lucky enough to achieve, really has to do with what they taught me. They really gave me an unbelievable value system.

GW: And you have always loved glamor.

DB: I love glamor. I was always interested in being in the theater or being a designer. I remember my parents going out and the parties at my house. Watching my mother and her friends all dressed up, the smell of perfume, the sound of their high heels on the wood floor—that was unbelievable. I was very mature as a young child.

GW: Did you study fashion in college?

DB: Yes, I studied at the Fashion Institute of Technology. But becoming a fur designer was purely by accident. I had worked for several houses on Seventh Avenue as a design assistant and was looking for a new job. I found one with a furrier. And I fell in love, it was so glamorous being around such a high-priced product. So I went in there, and I designed the collection, which was a big success. And several years into it, I went off on my own, in 1983. I took a little showroom and did a big fashion show at the Regency Hotel—the very next day Ivana Trump came in and bought seven coats. I've swathed them all—from Barbara Walters to Diana Ross.

GW: But does one really need a degree in fashion to be a fur designer, when all it requires is draping some dead muskrat over some hag calling herself a socialite?

DB: I feel that I *design* a collection. Many of the old-time fur designers or fur companies would think a mink coat should only look a certain way, but we're incorporating ready-to-wear. Ultimately, I will probably have a complete evening-wear collection because, you know, I love the night. I love the evening.

GW: And your charm, personality, and wit all add to the equation.

DB: Thank you. I *am* trying to have a good time. I'm from the school of the glass is half full.

GW: And the hair?

DB: The hair is natural. I call it couture silver.

GW: And what is considered the most luxurious animal one could possibly wear?

DB: To wrap yourself in the finest Russian sable is so gorgeous and so luxe—$150,000 and you are ready to go.

GW: And your statement to PETA would be?

DB: We live in America, and that is why we are here, because it is the greatest country in the world. They have their feelings and mission, and we have ours. We are not hurting anyone—we're working in one of the finest professions in the world. Our industry has been very supportive of numerous charities, and we should be commended for it.

Ivanka Trump

{ IVANKA TRUMP }

G W is so proud of Ivanka Trump! And despite all the naysayers—that fact is undisputable.

I have known Ivanka since she was a tween cavorting in her mother's closet, traipsing, or rather stumbling, around in Ivana's Manolo Blahniks, her lips pasted with her mum's expensive red lipstick. Who could have imagined that Ivanka would have evolved into a truly classic, incredible wife, mother, and now, even beyond her wildest dreams, First Daughter of the United States!—having been uniquely integral to the core coterie that helped her father become elected as forty-fifth president of the United States. One can only hope that Ivanka will truly evolve to be one of the core confidantes that will keep POTUS 45 grounded. We remain optimistic that Ivanka especially will be able to calm POTUS 45 at the moments when he seems to be morphing into a grotesque ogre of a Gila monster—worse than the Loch

Ness! We hope Ivanka will one day succeed. And that's no covfefe, honey bunny.

When we did this interview, in Ivanka's office at the eponymous Trump Tower in 2008, 'Vanka (as she is affectionately known in these parts) swanned down to the lobby to personally greet GW. Just the sight of this alpha fox peering down at me in her toe-cleavage Stuart Weitzman stiletto heels was enough to make me go butterfly weak. And looking back, I also feel even more proud that I insisted, after their initial breakup, that she reconcile with the man who would become her husband and the perfect father to her ever-growing brood.

IT: I was thinking as I was waiting how I have known you since I was fourteen.

GW: And I was thinking how proud I am of your effortless segue into the cultural zeitgeist. I just hope you are not spreading yourself too thin, 'Vanka. You seem to be juggling many different projects.

IT: No, I don't think I am spreading myself too thin. I make a cognitive effort to turn down those things that don't really excite me. Real estate is my main focus, and I'm loving it. *Forbes* just wrote that I am the youngest director on a publicly traded company in America. And I also do my jewelry, but that is a small business relative to the real estate.

GW: And you also design the uniforms for your hotel staff.

IT: Well, that is because I am literally involved with every detail of my hotel operations. I am trying to set a tone for the brand, so you really want to create a feeling. I am designing them because I know what I want a doorman at a five-star hotel to look like. I also do the interiors for all our hotels. Everything. Right down to picking out the china. The flat-screens.

GW: What is your official title here in the Trump Kingdom?

IT: I am vice president of development and acquisitions for the Trump Organization. I am president of Ivanka Trump Jewelry. And I am on the board of directors of Trump Entertainment Resorts.

GW: I am so impressed by the way you have come into your own, 'Vanka!

IT: I have always known I wanted to follow in my father's footsteps, but you never know until you actually do it if you are going to be any good. I now have that level of comfort where I know that I am good at what I do and that I can really enjoy it.

GW: Are you creating the rings for your mum's wedding this April?

IT: That's a good question. I did design the engagement rings, but she hasn't asked.

GW: Tell me about your daily morning ritual. What's the first thing you do when you get up?

IT: The first thing I do when I get up is to read the *New York Post*.

GW: What about your morning beauty rituals?

IT: Lately I've been using La Mer. I do have hundreds of bath products, and I really don't wear too much makeup. My bathtub is teeming with washes and scrubs.

GW: 'Tis a pity it was not to be a double wedding at Mar-a-Lago.

IT: I have enough on my plate, my God.

GW: If there is one vice, what would it be?

IT: I love to live in a free, casual way. I think big picture, but I sometimes get too obsessed with minor details, and I always have to remind myself not to. But I think part of the beauty of being twenty-six is still trying to figure out what life is all about. It is certainly not about drugs or alcohol, but there are a few personality flaws that I am looking into.

GW: You're so perfect, 'Vanka! Do you ever feel that you constantly try to measure up to your incredible mother and, of course, your larger-than-life father? I would be scared shitless to have "The Donald" as my dad.

IT: No. If I were to use my parents as any sort of measuring tool I would be in for a very bitter and hard and long road.

GW: Tell me the three warning signs any apprentice ought to know on "how to spot a frenemy."

IT: One is: Never allow yourself to be used. Make sure not to surround yourself with people whose only interest is what you can do for them. Be generous with your friends but not in a way where they are living off of you. Another sign to watch for is insincerity. Watch the way they react and treat you, and then watch the way they react and treat people they probably consider not as important as you. Duplicity is a key sign of the frenemy.

GW: 'Vanka, "the Force" is with you!

{ CARRIE DONOVAN }

AUGUST 1998

L et's face a few simple facts, the likes of Vanessa Friedman can't hold a candle to the *New York Times Styles* legend Carrie Donovan who was the indomitable doyenne of fashion critics for more than forty years.

Carrie was the queen of fashion critics and hence one of the world's most influential fashion journalists for decades. Yes, Carrie was from an era when the fashion critic really mattered. Yes, she was from before the era when social media ambushed and continues to rampage the fashion zeitgeist of the twenty-first century. And yes, she was from a generation where everyone seemed to be, and still is, a fashion critic or influencer, as they liked to call themselves. So Vanessa is no Carrie, but then again neither was Cathy Horyn. When it comes to famous fashion critics out of the *New York Times* there remains only one legend—Carrie Donovan. The fashion doyenne had just been cast to star in the TV commercials for Old Navy back in 1998 when we sat to speak. I especially relished her Diana Vreeland musings. . . .

GW: Those Old Navy people now look very smart for casting you in their commercials, Carrie. Did you ever think when you were front row at the Carrousel du Louvre oohing and aahing at the latest Chanel fashion show that you would become a TV star?

CD: Never! But, my dear, back then there was no Old Navy. The thing that I do love most is that the commercials seem to give people pleasure. They stop me on the street, and they will say, "Are you the lady in the Old Navy commercials?" The delivery boy from the Food Emporium doubles over in laughter at the idea of me trying to do the hula.

GW: How do you prepare for those rigorous shoots, Carrie?

CD: I don't. But I'm exhausted when I'm done. I don't leave bed for two days after those shoots.

GW: Carrie Donovan is seventy-something but far from geriatric!

CD: Not seventy-something! I'm seventy! Mrs. Vreeland used to say the thing that made her maddest was the stories that referred to her as being in her seventies. "I'm not in my seventies, I am sixty-nine!" Which she was.

GW: When did you first meet DV?

CD: Ooh, in the fifties. I was a reporter at the *New York Times*. Then I went to work for her when she became editor of *Vogue*. She was like a mother to me, a marvelous friend. I remember the first time I had to have heart surgery and she got so upset that I had to go off to Texas. "Carrie, you can't go alone! They might cut off your leg!" She was always concerned about me.

GW: This wasn't the time on the operating table when you died and were miraculously brought back to life?

CD: No, that was another time. That was the time I had this mad idea of having my jowls removed. That's when I conked out on the table. I did die on the table; it's perfectly true. When I woke up, I was in the ICU at New York Hospital! That was the end of any attempt at that. So I say, live with the chins and jowls, my dear. I don't want to see another hospital until I'm out for good.

GW: Carrie, you haven't changed your look in a thousand years. Those overdone Chanel things that have been manacled to your wrists for at least fifty seasons!

CD: They are Chanel relics, but I only wear them for the cameras, because they are falling apart. Karl Lagerfeld gave them to me, and since they're lacquer, they are rather fragile. I don't know what I'll do when those bracelets go. But I think you do kind of develop a style, your uniform.

GW: So have you completely given up your degree as a fashionista?

CD: That was another time in my life, but of course I'm interested in it. I love reading Suzy Menkes in the *International Herald Tribune* during collection time. And

I still have dinner with Kal Ruttenstein [of Bloom-ingdale's], because he is so tuned in. And I would love to see Donna [Karan], but she is so big. She's become a mogul now.

GW: Carrie, I agree. "For me, it's about Paris, Milan, and Old Navy." But Club Monaco is the chicest fashion chain of the moment!

CD: There is no question; I find Club Monaco very inter-esting.

GW: And Magic is nowhere as fabulous as Dinky, the Taco Bell Chihuahua!

CD: Magic is my baby, but I adore that Taco Bell Chihua-hua. He is a dish.

{ GERALDO RIVERA }

JUNE 1997

G eraldo Rivera is still "Geraldo-ing"! Somehow, someway he has managed to be a news television perennial and standout personality. The fact that Geraldo has managed to be a relevant television presence (these days on Fox News) for decades in the highly competitive, shark-infested waters of the New York mediarati is to be commended. I first met him in 1997—and even back then we were talking about his twenty-seventh year in television—and that, one must note, was twenty years ago! And Geraldo is still hanging around.

GW: Your career in television spans twenty-seven years and counting. How are you feeling these days?

GR: It's funny, I remember endorsing the "Live fast, die young with a beautiful corpse" philosophy twenty-five years ago. I'm sort of embarrassed to still be around at fifty-three, going strong, because it's so unlikely, as Marty Berman—my longtime executive producer—has said, I've always stayed out late, played too hard, worked too hard, and yet I am thriving.

GW: What about your accomplishments?

GR: I think surviving at a certain level of achievement is a huge accomplishment. I'm very proud of a lot of the work I've done. I'm embarrassed by a lot of it too. But I've done more right than wrong.

GW: You have WABC–New York to thank.

GR: That's where it started. I was a notorious lawyer working with the Young Lords—the Puerto Rican equivalent of the Black Panthers—and I insisted that they take me on as their counsel, and they did. I was on TV as their spokesman, and someone from WABC saw me and said, "We're gonna make you a star."

GW: Geraldo's first scoop was the Zapruder film. Is that what put you on the map as a premier agent provocateur?

GR: My first big story was the Zapruder footage shown for the first time ever on national TV in 1975. And raising the possibility of a conspiracy to kill the thirty-fifth president. My Elvis story in 1979 was the biggest story on *20/20*.

GW: Why were you fired from ABC [in 1985]?

GR: I went up against Roone Arledge, the most formidable, wicked inside fighter in the news business. I was disloyal. I publicly lambasted [Roone], who had been my biggest supporter. He killed a story about the relationship between the Kennedy brothers and Marilyn Monroe. I complained bitterly about it. I went public to *People* magazine, and he said goodbye.

GW: That skinhead melee on your show in 1988, in which your nose was broken, was trash TV at its nadir.

GR: That was very spontaneous, and very violent. On one hand, I was the cover of *Newsweek* the same week George [H. W.] Bush was elected president. On the other hand, the negatives are so heavy I can barely carry them today.

GW: People often ask me if I think you had an affair with Denise Brown [sister to Nicole Simpson, wife of O. J. Simpson]. Once when I was a guest on your TV show, on your set, I couldn't help but notice the sexual frisson between you both. So did you?

GR: No, I did not. I'm a flirt, George. You've probably seen that frisson with others as well.

GW: I have to say, I often find myself dumbstruck whenever I catch sight of your gluteus maximus. You have the tightest buns of any fifty-year-old man I have ever seen.

GR: [Laughs] My mother says that is my best feature.

GW: How many Emmys do you have on your mantel, Geraldo?

GR: I have ten.

GW: Do you pack heat?

GR: From time to time.

GW: So you own a gun?

GR: I own several guns. I got the guns in the 1980s when there were a lot of kidnappings, and I kept the guns on board my boat, mostly.

GW: Folk often say Geraldo not only wants to report the story, he wants to be the story. . . .

GR: That is probably one of the reasons people believe I was having an affair with Denise Brown or Faye Resnick. I do live my stories.

GW: Lately you've been screaming about a particular network for not giving you the respect you think you deserve.

GR: Yes, NBC. My career has been like a roller coaster. Now I'm on one of the upswings, enjoying a grudging acceptance I haven't seen in a while. Being one of the wise men of my generation is my goal now. If I can just kind of keep a lid on all the volcanic aspects of my life, I have an opportunity.

GW: One last question. The JonBenét Ramsey murder mystery—do you think Daddy did it?

GR: I believe either Daddy did it and Mom is covering up for him or vice versa.

GW: It's a twisted world out there Geraldo. You keep letting them have it.

Kate Moss

$\left\{ \text{KATE MOSS} \right\}$

JANUARY 1994

The first time I met Kate Moss she was fresh off the boat and had been living in Manhattan for a mere seven weeks. A fashion photographer by the name of Michel Haddi had asked GW to stop by his studio on lower Fifth Avenue. "I have this new girl coming over," he said. "They call her a waif; her name is Kate. I am putting you in the shoot with her for British *GQ*." And sure enough this really, really thin, tiny, and really, really shy girl soon showed up on the set. It was Kate Moss. And so we did the shoot that day for British *GQ*. I had no idea that Kate Moss would go on to attain iconic fashion status that day I met the pale, skinny, and woefully shy English girl for the first time. We went on to become fairly fast friends, and I was the person who introduced Kate Moss to Johnny Depp that night in Café Tabac many, many years ago. Little did I know that night—when she walked into Tabac with Naomi

Campbell, and I grabbed her hand and marched her over to where Johnny Depp was sitting and prompted, "Johnny, this is Kate, and Kate, this is Johnny"—that these two would then go on to trash hotel rooms across the globe, what with their wild and tempestuous jet-setting relationship that lasted years. I did this interview with Kate Moss during Fashion Week of 1993 in New York City.

GW: Okay, Miss Moss, what do you say to your critics who call you a chain-smoking anorexic supermodel?

KM: Well, I'm not anorexic, but I am a chain-smoker. I try and eat three meals a day. I eat a big breakfast and dinner, and a small lunch. For breakfast I love eggs and bacon; for dinner, Italian food. And there is this brilliant transvestite Thai restaurant in Paris I love going to. It's so fabulous!

GW: And you love smoking your Marlboros. . . .

KM: I know. My mum says to me, "If I see another picture of you with a fucking Marlboro in your hand, I'm going to kill you."

GW: What did she say when she saw that picture of you wearing a transparent shift with black panties and no bra?

KM: She said, "You could at least have worn white knickers!"

GW: You have the longest hair of any supermodel around today.

KM: Probably, Naomi [Campbell] has got longer hair, but that doesn't really count.

GW: Yeah, one week she has short hair, the next it's down to her waist. She must have some magic formula.

KM: She has hair extensions.

GW: I know, I'm just kidding. [Both shriek with laughter.] Tell me about being discovered at JFK airport—I think that's so chic!

KM: Pan Am was on strike, and I'd been at the airport for three days when Sarah Doukas [head of Storm Model Management] saw me. She sent her brother over to talk to me.

GW: Now your brother, Nick, is a hot model, and your former beau, Mario Sorrenti, is a hot fashion photographer.

KM: Yes, I don't know about Nick being a model. I never thought he'd be a model. But I always thought Mario would be a top photographer.

GW: But I hear that you and Mario are no longer girlfriend and boyfriend. What happened?

KM: Um . . . well, we're just sort of having a break. He lives in London and I live in Paris.

GW: But London isn't that far from Paris, darling. Is this a trial separation?

KM: I dunno. You know how it is—relationships.

GW: What shoes did you like most this season in Paris?

KM: Vivienne Westwood and John Galliano's.

GW: Of all those other supergirls, which ones are you closest with?

KM: The super, super ones—Naomi and Christy [Turlington].

GW: And now you are a fellow millionairess. . . .

KM: I don't think about it. The best thing about money is sending my mum checks.

GW: What does your mother do?

KM: Nothing, really, at the moment; she used to be a barmaid but she got the sack.

GW: A barmaid?!

KM: Yes, for ages. She'll kill me for telling people. She doesn't want anybody to know.

GW: You should take her to the fashion shows.

KM: She came to Vivienne's last year.

GW: It's such a trend amongst you models to take Mother to work with you.

KM: I know. I think they saw, like one girl do it, and it's, like, "Why can't I take my mother with me?"

GW: Would your mum mind me asking what size bra you wear?

KM: I don't wear bras, really. I've got a couple of those Gossard Wonderbras. They are so brilliant, I swear, even I can get cleavage with them.

GW: You must hate people constantly referring to you as a waif.

KM: Yeah, I do. I'm sick of it. I hate it. It's been going on forever. It's so boring. I'm just a normal girl. Leave me alone!

{ ROSS BLECKNER }

The artist Ross Bleckner to this day still owns Truman Capote's old beach house on the East End of Long Island—and I have always been immensely envious of that fact. After all, it remains one of the most enviable pieces of real estate out there. But I like Ross Bleckner a lot. For GW he is the epitome of the born and bred New York City artist as bona fide celebrity. His alma mater is even NYU, so he is a native New Yorker in every sense of the word. And he was mentored by Sol LeWitt and Chuck Close!

GW: So, Ross Bleckner, your Wikipedia claims that you studied with Sol LeWitt and Chuck Close. Does that mean you interned for Sol and Chuck?

RB: No, George, that just means that when I went to college at NYU, they happened to be teaching there. And you know how it is, George—you kind of enter into a dialogue, and sometimes that dialogue lasts a long time, and it did with both of them. Of course Sol has passed away, but I knew him for many, many years.

GW: You first started going to the East End how long ago? And what has always intrigued you most about the Hamptons?

RB: Well, the greatest thing for me is that it is close to New York City and even though I used to be "upstate" in the Hudson Valley in the ideal dream farmhouse, I decided to make a clean break in Sagaponack. Here, I have close friends and privacy when I want it. I am here from the second week in May until around November, so for more than half the year, this is where you will find me.

GW: Do you keep a schedule when you are out here? Where do you shop for bagels?

RB: I never keep a schedule, and I never shop for bagels.

GW: You own Truman Capote's place, for Christ's sake! And GW is fucking envious! And amazingly, you bought it for peanuts—a mere $800,000 in 1990. Today, you could easily sell that property to some bored oligarch for more than $40 million!

RB: That would be nice, trust me. I would be happy to sell it to some oligarch.

GW: What is it about that iconic piece of East End real estate that screamed *I have to own it?*

RB: It just happened to be available. It was just one of those circumstances.

GW: And you entertain here? And do you allow public tours of your studio?

RB: No and no. I never entertain here, but my friends can come over, sure, and I will serve them one bottle of Poland Spring water.

GW: Well, you were born under the sign of Taurus, after all. And you know what they say about Taurus men: They tend to be very stubborn and are creatures of habit. And most important of all: They are very, very cheap! Describe your work in general terms. What is it you seek?

RB: My paintings have a lot to do with consciousness and microcosm and looking out at the architecture in the sky, and looking at the mind and the body and the place where all that intercepts.

GW: Hence, some of your best-known works, where you have incorporated the use of your brain scans.

RB: I believe if you look at something close enough and long enough, it all becomes abstract.

GW: And how successful was your recent show at the Mary Boone Gallery? Were you happy with the reception to this year's first shown works in many, many years?

RB: Yes, I was very happy. Most of the pieces have sold, and I felt good about the work.

GW: I am sure if anyone has seen the much talked about, much buzzed, finally finished, brand-new home of your BFF Calvin Klein, it would be you, Ross Bleckner. Is it a modernist, jaw-dropping masterpiece?

RB: It is actually very simple and romantic and very much

the essence of Calvin. It is completely in line with his aesthetic, with an abundance of natural light.

GW: Is there going to be a huge bacchanal there this summer?

RB: No, those days are over.

GW: You know, I always remember the summer of Calvin and Nick a few seasons or three ago. The first time I saw them together at some posh event in Water Mill, I thought to myself, Wow. I love the way they complement each other. The chemistry was so natural—Nick Gruber was clearly being groomed to be a younger and gorgeous version of his sugar daddy. But they were a great couple! I think Calvin should give Nick another chance. I know Nick well and despite his erratic behavior, I like him a lot.

RB: Well, that is never going to happen. That is so over.

GW: And like Calvin Klein, you also have a twink fetish, or so the rumor goes.

RB: A what?

GW: A twink fetish—you prefer the company of much younger men!

RB: [Laughs uproariously] Hah! That is not at all true. At all.

GW: Is there any significant other in your life?

RB: I have a boyfriend, and he is no twink.

GW: One thing you love doing on a flawless sun-swept Saturday afternoon in Sagaponack would be what?

RB: Working in my studio more often than not, and I like to visit Wainscott a lot for some reason. I also like going to the beach, but I will not tell you which one. [Admiring my penmanship] Gosh, I love the way you write. No one can understand it.

GW: But that is the entire point, Ross. This is the GW version of hieroglyphs! Only GW can translate his entire penmanship. It is done on purpose. That said, do you feel that you are in your most creative fecund of late?

RB: I am always inspired when I go out to Long Island for the summer, and I am actually looking forward very much to what the rest of the season holds as far as my creative fecund as you call it [laughs uproariously]. I have been putting together a lot of ideas that I will explore in the open air of Sagaponack.

GW: I think you need to loosen up and sex up the next big projects, Ross Bleckner. Your work is way too dense for my personal tastes. I don't really get it, to be quite honest. Maybe that is why as your own longtime gallery guru Mary Boone says, "Ross is an artist's artist." I think you need to take a field trip to Venice for some adventurous inspiration.

RB: I'd love to, and I will take you up on that suggestion, but after the summer—it is way too hot and touristy now. As for not "getting my work," there is not much to get. Yes, it is very layered and very evocative of the elusive light source. But that's just my way of making you think.

GW: You resurrected Op art in the 1980s, according to one astute art critic. What would be your ethos or raison d'être for your twenty-first-century work?

RB: I would say that it will encompass a certain fragility and at the same time, a certain agility, and that is all I will say for now.

GW: Another fascinating factoid: Back in the eighties, Ross Bleckner lived in an apartment right above the legendary Mudd Club. The Mudd Club is the reason I decided I just had to move to New York City. I will never forget how star-struck and overcome with joy I was when I first walked into that hovel. For there across the room were Andy Warhol and Keith Haring. I was just giddy with glee.

RB: Yes, I did live above the Mudd Club, and yes, I am not surprised you saw Keith Haring there, because he used to work there at the time. I was never friends with Andy Warhol. I always thought he was a bit of a creep. And to be quite honest, even though I lived above the Mudd Club, I hardly ever went there.

GW: And why is it that most of your works are titled "Untitled"? That all sounds so forced and pretentious. Why is it that hard just to throw a title on a completed painting.

RB: Because I like the idea of the person viewing my work to come up with their own ideas, their own thoughts on what that work means and as such what they would want to call it. I guess that all just defines the essence of my ambiguity.

Sandra
Bernhard

{ SANDRA BERNHARD }

I did this interview with the comedienne Sandra Bernhard in the summer of 1988. It was one of my first big celebrity "gets." At the time Sandra Bernhard was a hot commodity and best friends with Madonna. Her brilliant one-woman show, *Without You I Am Nothing*, was a hit Off-Broadway that year, and the tart-tongued comic gave this interview that helped launch my career as the modern master of the celebrity question and answer.

During that summer of 1988 Sandra and Madonna had tongues wagging all over town with their Sapphic hijinks. The girlfriends had been introduced by the ex-husband [Sean Penn] of the then empress of pop culture [Madonna] in the home of her then new boyfriend [Warren Beatty].

For some reason Sandra Bernhard and Madonna bonded and were virtually inseparable for years to follow. . . .

GW: When I saw you in Santa Monica a month ago you told me you were on your way to Las Vegas for your debut at Bally's. How did that go?

SB: To be honest with you I don't remember. I was working harder than Liza Minnelli and Judy Garland put together. I was busting my ass up there just to keep it going.

GW: When are you inspired to write your material?

SB: I write in a kind of unusual way because I have a collaborator, John Boskovich. So, usually he will think up a new song or an old song, and we will sit down with the band and sort of start working. That's how we come up with the show. And of course there are a lot of times onstage when I am very spontaneous.

GW: You and Lypsinka were like the biggest hits at that Thierry Mugler fashion gala at the Century Plaza the other day. That APLA [AIDS Project Los Angeles] fashion extravaganza was everything!

SB: Yes, I know. It was a real exciting night!

GW: I was standing backstage that night and Sharon Stone must have passed me a million times and I didn't recognize her once.

SB: You didn't? Well, she's not really that distinctive, if you know what I mean. She is not really unusual looking.

GW: Every story I have ever read about you always has one word to describe Sandra Bernhard—"ambiguous."

SB: I hate being pigeonholed, but what else are they going to call me? In terms of my sexuality, I've always been pretty much open. At the moment I'm involved with a woman, and I will probably continue to be involved with women. I've had a new girlfriend for the last two months, but I think she would rather have her name private.

GW: Speaking of ambiguous. How is your friend David Letterman doing?

SB: Hah! You are funny! That's brilliant! I think I may be doing his show again when I get back to New York. The last time I checked on him was right after the New Year and he was in good spirits. He has his niche. You can't touch David Letterman. I think right now, of all the people with talk shows, he is the most solid. He is most true to himself. He doesn't try to please the audience.

GW: I love your loyalty. Are you booked to do the Jay Leno show anytime soon?

SB: No. I'm not really featuring Jay. I adore Letterman and Arsenio is really comfortable with himself and has a lot of fun with his gig. I don't need to go hopping from talk show to talk show.

GW: So what is it about Jay Leno that so gets on your nerves?

SB: I've known Jay for years. He's just okay. I think he interrupts his guests too much.

GW: And what do you think about Dennis Miller?

SB: I think he is just another smug asshole. Just another know-it-all white man.

GW: And didn't you pose nude for *Playboy*?

SB: Yes. I posed nude for *Playboy* and I have the September cover.

GW: You were totally and completely nude?

SB: Yeah! I mean, you are not looking up straight into my pussy. It's not a gynecological exam, but you do see my red pubic hair, which everyone is always delighted to see.

GW: Are you really that comfortable with your body?

SB: Yes, I really am. I feel great about my body. I work out at Gold's Gym in West Hollywood with an incredible trainer by the name of Luis de Freitas. He's Brazilian and was Mr. World in 1986. He's great. I work out with him four days a week. I love it, but it's not like I'm going around preaching it. I'm not obsessed with it, but it has helped my body a lot.

GW: You've become the hip AIDS charity hostess of late. You are quite involved with a lot of AIDS charities.

SB: I guess I am but I am not just doing this for publicity.

GW: And you were on that stage in the rain during the APLA event looking flawless in Isaac Mizrahi.

SB: When you think about the people who have AIDS and are suffering from it, what is it for me to go out in the misty night for an hour. Big fucking deal. And fashion is one of my first loves. I think if I had been ten years younger, I would have had a modeling career.

GW: Well, look at Kristen McMenamy. She is the new runway star and she is almost the spitting image of you with that sneer.

SB: I know! When I saw a video of a show last year that she was in I said, "God, that girl looks just like me!" It is so exciting.

GW: So it's been a long-held dream to be a model?

SB: Yes. I wanted to do that more than anything. But now I get to be in a few shows and that is very exciting. I love fashion. The last time I was on Arsenio I wore this beautiful, sheer Vivienne Westwood with big valley hair. It was really cool. I love Vivienne Westwood.

GW: What is the one thing you could never get used to about Hollywood?

SB: I guess the extreme phoniness.

GW: The typical Hollywood cliché.

SB: Yes! But it's true! I'm not talking about everybody in Hollywood, but it's really true. I'm not good at schmoozing the show business world. I can do it with the fashion world where the people are more enlightened. But people in the showbiz world don't have a lot to say.

GW: And now to the Madonna question. I hear the friendship between the two of you has cooled of late and that you really don't speak to each other anymore. Word is that you are so over Madonna because of the way she flirted outrageously with the girl you brought with you to her New Year's Eve party last year.

SB: No. I'm not mad at Madonna. But I guess things have cooled a bit between us. A lot of interesting things have taken place over the year that have been out of the realm of my comprehension. So I really don't know what's going on.

GW: Well, clarify the situation, Sandra. Are you over Madonna or what?

SB: It is too complicated and it is too personal.

GW: One can assume though that you are not on the telephone every day indulging in babe talk.

SB: No. We are not.

GW: How did you and Roseanne Barr become such good friends?

SB: I met her a year and a half ago at Sue Mengers's house. We started talking and we really hit it off. We share the same point of view about Hollywood. She is a real down-to-earth person and the next thing I know she called me to do her show.

GW: And now you are a regular on *Roseanne*.

SB: I play a character called Nancy who is supposed to be marrying Tom Arnold's character. I start taping for the new season at the end of August.

GW: Tell GW the one phrase that best sums the philosophy of Sandra Bernhard?

SB: Cast your fate to the winds.

{BOB COLACELLO}

I will always revere the star journalist Bob Colacello for being one of my earliest supporters—one of the very first New York City legends to champion my cause and provide moral support to follow my dreams. I remember being in boarding school and reading Bob Colacello's genius work as a major editor at *Interview* magazine. So for me to meet him and then be mentored by this magazine legend was nothing I could have ever imagined.

Bob was a huge fan of my Xerox magazine, *R.O.M.E.* And he would always take me to dinner in those early days when I was living on Mamoun's falafel sandwiches and pizza. He would often treat me to dinner at Da Silvano's because he knew how much I loved the Italian fare there and could never afford it. I did this interview with him for *R.O.M.E.* because he had just released his new book, *Holy Terror: Andy Warhol Close Up*. And I was thrilled because he was one of the first influencers ever to tell me that my little Xerox-copy-machine-printed magazine, *R.O.M.E.*, was "absolute genius"—his very own words.

We met in Caffe Dante on MacDougal Street. I was so excited to get a signed copy of his book. Because if there was one who could claim to be the official biographer to the court of Warhol—it would have to be Bob Colacello!

He was hired by Andy Warhol in 1970 and went on to mold *Interview* magazine into prominence while becoming, along with Fred Hughes, one of the artist's two closest confidantes. When he left *Interview* in 1983, he had gathered enough material to write ten books. He began work on *Holy Terror* a week after Andy Warhol's sudden death in 1987 and he didn't finish it for another three years.

"Andy wanted to be the official portrait painter of the ruling classes," he told me as we sat for espresso at the iconic MacDougal Street café. Here I was, completely awestruck sitting before the king of pop journalism for one of my very earliest interviews. . . .

GW: So you are really up there now "Count Valpolicella." Life must be even more ultra-fabulous for you than it has ever been.

BC: It was never that fabulous, was it?

GW: Oh, you know it was! Are you relieved the book is finally complete and finally published?

BC: Yes, I am. Three years playing the recluse is not an easy role for me. And it's just fun to walk by a bookstore and see it in the windows.

GW: I love that nickname, "Count Valpolicella," which was given to you by Salvador Dalí. Which chapter did you enjoy writing the most?

BC: Well, the Imelda [Marcos] chapter was fun to write because it was almost a Restoration comedy of errors. There were some days that I wrote twenty pages, and some days that I wrote half a page. It was a hard book to write because I realized in order to write about Andy and the whole period that he was so much a center of I had to write about myself a lot. I couldn't say that Elsa Peretti took too much cocaine one night at Studio 54 without saying that I was also doing it with her. I thought if I was going to be honest as I could about everybody else, I had to be honest about myself. And then having made that decision, I thought, God, do I really want to do this. Am I going to make a fool of myself?

GW: Some critics have concluded that *Holy Terror* is the *Mommie Dearest* of Warhol sagas. *Time* magazine has even called it a "get-even book."

BC: My motto as a journalist has always been: no hatchet jobs and at the same time no puff pieces. *Time* magazine is the *Mommie Dearest* of newsweeklies. I read *The Economist*.

GW: I have to tell you that Victor Hugo is thoroughly pissed with you. He hated his portrayal in the book and he personally told me the book "was nothing but trash."

BC: That's not what he said to me at the book party. He

said, "Darling, I love it, including everything you said about me."

GW: Well, he told me it was trash one late night when I ran into him at the Limelight. So, Victor is obviously still a total mess.

BC: Victor gave me an interview for the book. I asked Halston to give me an interview, and Victor Hugo was there when I went to interview Halston. And it was after Andy died but before the diaries came out, so it wasn't a spiteful interview.

GW: Was this the "Organza" interview in the book?

BC: The "Organza" thing was Halston's way of gossiping about whatever it was that Andy was doing in the bathroom between the orgy photo sessions which were arranged by Victor for the sex paintings which Andy was working on at the time. And Victor collaborated with him on that project. And Victor deserves credit for getting Andy to put down on canvas what a large part of the seventies were about. It was about extreme sexual experimentation. It was about the sexual revolution coming through.

GW: Victor told me that you were nothing more than a Warhol lackey and that you kissed so much ass that your tongue was virtually all the way up Andy's asshole. That is what Victor Hugo said to me about you at the Limelight!

BC: Well, Victor has a very colorful way of speaking, which is kind of half Venezuelan and half West Village. I like Victor. Sometimes, Victor drove me crazy. It was hard when we were trying to run a business there. We had to have limits and constraints and Victor is not the sort of person you can limit. But nobody ever did better windows than the ones Victor did for Halston—nobody! Victor Hugo was the Dalí of window design.

GW: How soon after starting to work for Warhol did you come to realize that maybe you could write a book about that experience one day?

BC: I have been keeping journals since 1967, notebooks on my experiences, so I was always keeping a diary when I first met Andy.

GW: How did the title *Holy Terror* come about?

BC: I interviewed a lot of people in Pittsburgh, which is where Andy was born: his brothers, many of his cousins, some of his neighbors. And one neighbor, whose parents rented Andy's parents' apartment where Andy was born said, "Oh, Andy was a real holy terror when he was two or three years old. He used to kick his mother in the shins." And I just thought that Andy was a holy terror even as a grown-up. Then there is also the religious imagery. Andy went to church every Sunday as an adult. That was the holy part.

GW: What's some of the juicier stuff that got cut out of the book?

BC: A lot of what was cut was just funny stories that basically made the same point about other funny stories. So we tried to choose the funniest. Sylvia Miles and Joe Dallesandro at the Cartagena Film Festival with

Joe threatening to walk into the Atlantic because
Sylvia wouldn't come into his room.

GW: You mean Sylvia wouldn't do it with Joe? She spurned
the gorgeous Joe Dallesandro?!

BC: Sylvia is quite respectable under that bohemian image
of hers. A lot of what we cut was stuff that was too
much about other people and not enough about Andy.
Grace Jones's alleged affair with Glenn O'Brien was
also cut out of the book.

GW: This book seems tailor-made for celluloid.

BC: No, it wasn't actually, although a big-name producer
did approach me and offer to option the book if I said
that Andy was straight before Edie [Sedgwick] died.
That was the Hollywood approach. I couldn't think
about doing that.

GW: Who would you want to play you if there was ever a
Hollywood movie version of your *Holy Terror*?

BC: Tom Cruise. I think there are two people who could
play Andy well . . . Willem Dafoe and John Malkovich.

GW: I think Crispin Glover would have the upper hand
since he is playing Andy Warhol in the upcoming
Oliver Stone movie about The Doors.

BC: Fred [Hughes] also wants Tom Cruise to play him in
the movie. We would have to fight it out!

GW: I have only one disappointment with the book. You
still didn't tell us how Andy's everlasting quote,
"Everyone will be famous for fifteen minutes," ever
came about.

BC: Well, I wasn't there when it came about. It comes

from a 1967 interview that Andy did in Sweden. But when Andy did interviews in the seventies, he would always have Fred or me or somebody sitting next to him, to help him with his answers. So, for all I know, those words could have come from Gerard Malanga. Most of Andy's interviews were done with someone sitting by his side helping him out.

{ IAN SCHRAGER }

I an Schrager—the visionary impresario who created Studio 54 (with his partner Steve Rubell) and then reinvented and created the concept of the boutique hotel—was in the middle of yet another fabulous party that he orchestrated. He had just transformed the lobby of his Paramount Hotel in midtown Manhattan into an elegant dining hall and was hosting a party with Anna Wintour of *Vogue* fame for three of Europe's leading fashion designers: Christian Lacroix, Karl Lagerfeld, and Gianni Versace.

It had been the most buzzed-about party amongst the Manhattan *bon chic, bon genre* for weeks. And as they swanned in to the Paramount Hotel that night, the first person they saw was the legendary impresario himself who stood at the entrance to greet all the fashion bessies.

"I am an entertainer who doesn't entertain, a fashion designer who doesn't make clothes," were his first few words as I moved in to say hello. "I am always trying to inspire the tastemakers," he followed in that familiar Brooklynese lisp of an accent.

Ian Schrager gave up his law profession to open a nightclub in 1977, and now more than twenty years later he was cooing about his latest jewel "and the first luxury hotel at popular prices" in the world. The opening of the Paramount had completed the troika of the first chic boutique hotels in New York City. That is, Morgans, the Royalton, and now the Paramount.

"Nightclubs were the center of social activity in New York in the nineteen-seventies," he reasoned. "Restaurants served that function in the eighties, and hotel lobbies are going to be the definitive social hub of the nineteen-nineties." Today, in 2017, he opens his first hotel and condominium bearing his name. But back in 1994, he was very much at the vanguard of this new movement . . . the boutique hotel concept.

GW: I cannot believe that you haven't been asked to be in one of those GAP print ads?

IS: [Laughs] I have been asked three times to be in the GAP campaign and I have said no each time. Herb Ritts himself called me a couple of weeks ago to do one. But the only reason I go out in public is to talk about my work. I don't want to be a public persona. I only talk about myself because I am talking about my work.

GW: Isn't this new hotel of yours going to cannibalize the Royalton, which is only minutes away by taxicab.

IS: No. The Royalton and Morgans are my apples and

this is my orange. This is a six-hundred-room hotel and some people don't want to stay in a six-hundred-room hotel. The Royalton is a small luxury hotel and the Paramount is a big, dynamic hotel.

GW: Can you remember the first time you met Steve Rubell?

IS: I remember it precisely. I met him when I went to college in 1964 at Syracuse University. I was having an underwear fight, wrestling another guy by the name of Marty Goldstein. We were both horsing around in our underwear. Steve was a senior and I was a freshman. So I was having this underwear fight and I was losing but I wouldn't give up, and I think Steve took note of that. And we just became friendly and we were friends from that day forward in the fall of 1964.

GW: What are some of the plans involving Paramount that will come to define the new cool scene here?

IS: We will have a Brian McNally restaurant and a collaboration with the famous Les Bains Douches nightclub in Paris. It's going to be an elegant supper club, not a dance club. I don't want a million kids waiting outside to get in. I do want it to restart New York nightlife again because the city needs it.

GW: I was just about to get on that subject. New York City nightlife seems moribund. What the hell has happened to the great NYC nightlife? Do you think the mayor [Dinkins] is killing nightlife in the city?

IS: There are problems with drugs and crime but they are not responding in the right way. Nightlife is important to a great city. Every great city has great nightlife. Barcelona has a stylish bar on every corner and the same with Hong Kong. New York used to be like that but not anymore. If you take away the nightlife of New York City, then you take away one of the great, essential ingredients about the city, so this Dinkins administration does have to be a bit more sensitive. And secondly, the young promoters coming up, the young impresarios must not be afraid or apprehensive about creating and opening nightclubs.

GW: What nightclubs have you been to recently?

IS: The other night I went to almost all of them. I needed to see the scene elsewhere. I went to Le Palace and I went to Rex and The Building.

GW: Which one did you like the best?

IS: I liked The Building on Sixth Avenue. But you know there was no glamor, no mix. I didn't see the tuxedos dancing next to those in jeans or jeans dancing with ballgowns.

GW: How did the passing of Steve Rubell affect you?

IS: It was a big loss but so was losing my father and my mother and my sister. Losing Steve was a big loss. He was my best friend and I will never get over these losses.

GW: Was he sick before he went into the hospital?

IS: No, he wasn't. Steve went into the hospital with every intention of coming out of there. It's unfortunate that in this day and age that if you are under ninety and die that everyone thinks you died of AIDS.

GW: Are you saying that you don't believe that Steve Rubell died of AIDS?

IS: Precisely! I knew everything about Steve Rubell. If he had AIDS, there would be no reason for me to say that he didn't die from it.

GW: What do you think about Donald Trump?

IS: I'm a big fan of Donald Trump. I think he is brilliant. What he does is not my individual taste, but he was good for New York, and he was larger-than-life and New York needs more Donald Trumps, not less Donald Trumps. I am a big fan of his. It's great having a lot of talented, flamboyant people doing great things in a big city.

GW: What did you learn from your experience in jail. You spent thirteen months in jail for tax problems.

IS: Well, I learnt that I am thankful for having been given the opportunity for another chance. I learnt that the system works, and I am not an outlaw anymore. I'm not a crook. I've learnt that you can play by the rules and it won't stifle your creativity. But basically, it taught me humility. And it has given me more enthusiasm. I have learnt how to deal with success and failure. And let me tell you—I much prefer dealing with the success.

GW: Are you a restless individual?

IS: I am. I have a fire inside but I have been getting more at peace with myself as I grow older. I have mellowed. It used to be I was only happy when I was working but that is not the case anymore.

{ TONY CURTIS }

I remember being thrilled to bits the day I interviewed Tony Curtis back in the early years of the twenty-first century. That very same morning, I picked up the *New York Daily News*, only to find myself reading about myself in an especially fabulous Liz Smith syndicated column.

"George Wayne, whose monthly Q&A in *Vanity Fair* has caused stars to curse, hang up, threaten Wayne's life and otherwise wonder what the hell they got themselves into . . ." she wrote. Thank God Liz forgot to send Tony Curtis the memo, I thought to myself later that afternoon as I sat to speak with yet another Hollywood legend. This Tony Curtis, the well-noted Hollywood boulevardier, the actor who was married three times. The actor who will live in celluloid history for his most famous role, dressing in drag to land Marilyn Monroe in *Some Like It Hot*.

GW: Where did you get that nickname "Bonnie" from?

TC: Sinatra gave me the name.

GW: They could open a library to house all the movies you've appeared in.

TC: One hundred and twenty.

GW: I thought it was one hundred and thirty.

TC: Fifteen of those were child-support payments.

GW: Most of them are unwatchable. Which are your all-time favorites?

TC: *Some Like It Hot, Sweet Smell of Success, Spartacus, The Outsider, The Vikings, The Boston Strangler.*

GW: What was the last movie you were in?

TW: It was called *The Continued Adventures of Reptile Man,* about two years ago, but it didn't get much distribution. I'm not that interested in films anymore.

GW: You got lucky with your career. Did you really want to be an actor?

TC: I wanted to be in the movies. I wanted to be a movie star. And it happened for me. Isn't that fabulous?

GW: A career that spanned decades.

TC: I've always dedicated myself to my profession. I love being a movie star. I'm as privileged as anybody in the world can be. I'm handsome, I'm wealthy, and I have a beautiful thirty-year-old wife. And now I have this opportunity to do a play. Can you imagine, at seventy-seven years old? I'm starting out on a brand-new career.

GW: The Library of Congress has called *Some Like It Hot* a national treasure.

TC: I can be candid with you—it is.

GW: I read somewhere that you said, "Kissing Marilyn Monroe was like kissing Hitler."

TC: Never said it! It's all bullshit. It all happened when Marilyn was at her most difficult time. And the studio was so angry with her they put her on suspension. Marilyn and I were lovers in 1950. She went much too quickly. The biggest woman star in the business and she was living like a bag woman. There was no one to look after her. Where were all her friends? Why wasn't anyone with her after she had tried to kill herself a few times before?

GW: So you did make whoopee with Marilyn!

TC: Yes. We were on for a few months. We were in our twenties. There was nothing special or unique about it.

GW: How many of the leading ladies did you bed?

TC: I bedded every leading lady except one—Jack Lemmon.

GW: Didn't you do Cary Grant?

TC: No, no, I did not. There was no carnal relationship at all.

GW: You've been a Hollywood stud for decades and you never had a homo affair?

TC: What are you talking about? No, no, never did. I attracted a lot of gay friends, but I never had any inclination. Rock Hudson was a great friend; he and I started at Universal together. That just never happened. I was what you call pussy-whipped.

GW: Tony, what's the first thing to go at seventy-five? Have you had a testicle tuck?

TC: No, no, I have had nothing tucked. In a year or two I plan to do a little facial work. I had to have some work done to my nose, but that was for a deviated septum from too much cocaine.

GW: What's breakfast like for Tony Curtis?

TC: Going to McDonald's and having a bagel with sausage, egg, and cheese. Once in a while I do that. Usually it's a grapefruit and cereal. At dinnertime I love to take my beautiful wife out and really live it up.

GW: I was just about to ask you about the glamazon. Where did you meet this fifth wife?

TC: Having dinner with some guy. I went up and introduced myself to the guy. I never looked at her until halfway through the conversation. She told me she was an equestrian with a riding school. And I asked her where her stable was, "May I have your number?" Right under this guy's nose.

GW: Most of your peers are six feet under.

TC: That makes me so sad. Grant, Gable, Lancaster. Gary Cooper was a wonderful man to be around. Marilyn, Rosalind Russell, Natalie Wood. We would all call each other, and have dinner occasionally. I don't see that or hear that anymore, and it makes me sad.

GW: Whom do you miss the most?

TC: Jack Lemmon was the best fucking man.

GW: Well, what can I say: What becomes a legend most? You, Tony Curtis!

Charlton Heston

{ CHARLTON HESTON }

T ake your paws off me, you damn dirty ape!" That is all I kept thinking to myself in this classic GW Q&A with the LEGEND of Hollywood legends! The one and only Charlton Heston. The thought came on as he rambled on. And those, of course, were the classic words he uttered so unforgettably in the 1968 legend called *Planet of the Apes*. Charlton Heston has starred in some of the greatest and most celebrated Hollywood movies of all time. Playing grand over-the-top titans like God and Moses and an alpha-male gladiator. So GW got to interview God in early 1994. And to this day, I consider this interview with Charlton Heston the greatest "get" of my career.

GW: Mr. Heston, do you mind if I call you Chuck?
CH: By all means . . .

GW: You've always been known for your larger-than-life roles: Moses, Ben-Hur, El Cid . . .

CH: Well, I challenge "larger-than-life." Most of those roles have been about specific historical individuals—Michelangelo, Richelieu, Moses. To call them larger-than-life means they are not real people.

GW: But were you not the first action hero—before Stallone or Schwarzenegger?

CH: I guess you could describe *Ben-Hur* as an action film. In a sense, I think the action film has developed as a genre. *El Cid* was certainly an action film. No, I take back what I said about *El Cid*. Both *El Cid* and *Ben-Hur* are epics. That's the proper definition of those films.

GW: What roles are you getting these days?

CH: I'll soon be playing Brigham Young, who is to Mormons the Moses of his day. I am also in a film with Sam Neill called *In the Mouth of Madness*.

GW: You seem to be in tremendous physical shape for a senior citizen. What's your regime?

CH: I get up at 5:30 a.m. I read the paper, I have my toast and coffee, get in the pool, and I am out by 7:00. Then I play an hour of tennis.

GW: Are you a card-carrying member of the John Birch Society?

CH: Certainly not.

GW: But your politics are extremely conservative.

CH: My politics aren't far from the politics of the Democratic Party in the days of Jack Kennedy, for whom I campaigned.

GW: What are your thoughts on President Clinton?

CH: Let's not get into that.

GW: Okay. Is drinking malt whiskey your only vice?

CH: Yeah, well, I'm trying to stop that; as you grow older you have to quit all kinds of things you enjoy.

GW: For me there is not a more glorious image than that of a young Charlton Heston in a suit of chain mail. What role is your all-time favorite?

CH: It would either be Macbeth or Marc Antony. The great roles are always Shakespearean.

GW: Which of your leading ladies was it hardest having screen sex with?

CH: I don't see any advantage in saying negative things about any of them, but I turned down a picture with Marilyn Monroe because it was just going to be too difficult.

GW: Would you be up for a role in the sequel to *Planet of the Apes*?

CH: Oliver Stone says he wants to remake it, but I don't think I'd like to do that makeup again.

GW: What recent films have you liked?

CH: Many, but I'll tell you about one film I don't like: *The Piano*.

GW: Holly Hunter didn't impress you?

CH: Well, first of all, we never were told why she was mute. And one must always remember that playing someone mute is a surefire road to an Academy Award nomination.

GW: You must deal with awestruck strangers every day of your life.

CH: I am grateful that people like my work. They're very nice to me and I appreciate it. You have to recognize that what they are admiring in my case—I've played some extraordinary men. So it's hard not to think well of Moses and John the Baptist and those guys. Of course, that is not really me, but I try to be the kind of public man that does not deflate that reputation. But it's hard living up to Moses.

{ IVANA TRUMP }

OCTOBER 1993

I vana Trump, or "Godmama Ivana" as I would come to dub her over the years, grew to be a great friend and a patron of GW. But my first introduction to the grand and fabulous Ivana Trump was not in the shape or fashion I could ever have anticipated. My first introduction to Ivana Trump was back in the Big Eighties when she had her lawyers fire off a letter threatening to sue George Wayne because he had placed Ivana on his Worst-Dressed List. It's true! Ivana Trump wanted to sue GW. I said something silly like "Ivana has tacky style and needs a fashion overhaul" or something like that and she threatened to sue me! I still have the letter from her attorneys! Next to my file with the ones from Leonardo DiCaprio and Claudia Schiffer, who also were miffed at something GW said but quickly backed down when they clearly had a baseless case. But Ivana came to warm up to GW and soon came to be christened with the moniker "Godmama Ivana." She remains one of the most amazing people in my life. For a while there I was weekly invited to Ivana's mansion off Fifth Avenue for gossip and Veuve Clicquot champagne before we hit the town together. Her children, Ivanka and Eric, would pop in to give her a kiss good night as we were chauffeured all over uptown and downtown—the hot spots. A lot of the time we would do dinners at Nello or Serafina, which she still loves to this day. But I will never forget my very first dinner party with Ivana. I mean how could you forget a hostess who decides to go ahead with a festive dinner party on the very same night that the forty-first president of the United States, George Herbert Walker Bush, alerted the nation in a live press conference that he was sending America to war by invading Kuwait? Queen Bee Ivana did not care in the least and she went ahead with her fabulous dinner party, which was in the kitchen of the Plaza Hotel, which her husband Donald Trump then owned and where Ivana ruled as its grande dame. I will never forget that night—that eight-course meal in the executive kitchen with her young chef Kerry Simon and Ivana dressed to the nines with that fabulous helmet hair and Christian Lacroix couture frock and the jewels she turned out in! It was vintage Ivana!

GW: Is it difficult being a single mother nurturing three children?

IT: Not really, because my kids are really fabulous. They

are not spoilt—they could have been, but they are not. They are my best friends.

GW: You don't spoil your kids?

IT: Absolutely not. I teach them my values: not to cheat, steal, or lie, and not to take drugs and alcohol.

GW: When will Ivana take a third husband?

IT: I don't know. I just got a divorce, and I've been through hell. I don't need a man now for starting a family. I'm secure, and I am making my own life. I for sure don't need a man for prestige or career.

GW: Where did you meet your boyfriend Riccardo Mazzucchelli?

IT: We met two years ago in London.

GW: Is he a better lover than Donald?

IT: Oh, you know, that's very personal.

GW: I heard he likes to cook you pasta.

IT: Riccardo is a fabulous chef. I'm pretty good in the chicken paprika and goulash and all those European dishes with which you don't lose weight; I guarantee you Riccardo is excellent on pasta.

GW: Is Ivana a feminist?

IT: No. I have always been following the man. I was brought up like that, but in a good sense, to look to the man for decision-making and leadership. I am not a feminist, but I feel that I am equal definitely.

GW: I suppose you haven't worn polyester ever since you emigrated from Czechoslovakia?

IT: Well, I wear my polyester wet suit for scuba diving,

but don't say I haven't worn polyester since I left Czechoslovakia—sure I do.

GW: You have a new book, and you've been appearing on the Home Shopping Network. Tell me about that.

IT: The book is a sequel to my first book and is called *Free to Love*. I have just given my publishers my third book, which is a how-to book called *On My Own*. I've gotten over a million letters from women asking me for advice. It gave me the idea to go and answer them. [On TV] I'm selling my signature line of cosmetics—and something called mini-lift.

GW: Why do you think people won't admit they've had plastic surgery?

IT: I have no idea. It is not wrong or right. If you have a nose which you've hated all your life and you want to change it, great. If it doesn't matter to you, that's all right, too.

GW: Is Ivana a woman of the nineties?

IT: I think that you should be the judge of that. I'm contemporary. I'm the woman who wants it all.

GW: When all was said and done Donald did finally admit that you are a "special woman."

IT: Well, we are very good friends.

GW: Does Ivana wear fur?

IT: Not much, because it is being resented now. If it is a little chinchilla or a leopard or a jaguar which is endangered, that I can understand. But when you have the mink, which is grown like chicken or turkey, they are not endangered, and it wants to be worn, then I think that's great.

GW: Finish this sentence: Ivana be . . .

IT: . . . a happy person.

GW: I love you, Ivana.

{ KATHLEEN TURNER }

APRIL 2002

Kathleen Turner was a rather shocking sight to behold the day I interviewed her. Let's just say the Hollywood siren was looking nothing like the sultry Hollywood beauty we had grown accustomed to seeing on the big screen. She was appearing on Broadway in *The Graduate*, and all I kept thinking was, *What is her leading man going to do when he sees the blister on his costar's lip?*

GW: I was reading somewhere where someone called your London Mrs. Robinson a one-note performance.

KT: Oh, rubbish. The reviews were extraordinarily wonderful. We never had an empty seat. We broke all West End records.

GW: It should be easy trying to seduce Jason Biggs.

KT: I haven't been having any trouble so far.

GW: Once upon a time your movie career was on a roll: *Body Heat, Romancing The Stone, Prizzi's Honor, The Jewel of the Nile*. By the time *Peggy Sue Got Married* came around you were probably the most famous actress in the world.

KT: Oh, I was the biggest box-office woman in the world then!

GW: And then kaput! Your career went off a precipice.

KT: Oh, you know, I really don't understand why you talk like that! Unless you are trying to be provocative.

GW: Let's just face the facts, Katherine.

KT: Kathleen! The facts are that I have continued to work nonstop.

GW: In the nineties as compared to the eighties?

KT: After *Serial Mom*—

GW: Which—sorry—was your *Mommie Dearest*.

KT: Oh, you're wrong. Certainly in Europe it was a hugely successful film. Right after *Serial Mom*, I was diagnosed with rheumatoid arthritis. For several years that was my major battle. I did films that were not too demanding physically. They'd told me I was going to be in a wheelchair for the rest of my life. I said, "I don't think so." When I started to get more mobility, I came back to theater, mostly. It's time I got back in front of the camera, but, frankly, I love the theater.

GW: You and Betty Bacall should do a movie together, if only so we could hear the badinage between those two magical voices.

KT: We have such fun with our low voices every time we

meet. It's like, "Good evening, Miss Bacall." "Good evening, Miss Turner."

GW: Do you get recognized more by your voice than by your face?

KT: It's great when you want to get a reservation at a restaurant. I'll call up and say, "Hello, this is Kathleen Turner," and they say, "Yes, it is."

GW: When are you going to quit the cigarettes?

KT: I don't know. I guess I am going to have to someday. This character smokes, so it's not going to be now.

GW: What about your Tallulah Bankhead project?

KT: We did fourteen cities since last year and it went very well. But the script still needs work. When all this is done, I will go back to Tallulah because I really loved it. She is so flamboyant and so outrageous.

GW: How would you describe your approach to your craft?

KT: I don't think of myself as a method actor. A good script will give you all the information you need. Your job is to decide the thoughts to be conveyed, and the emotions to be felt—and to hit every one of those notes.

GW: Thank you, Miss Turner, for being such a good sport.

{ FARRAH FAWCETT }

OCTOBER 2000

I n the late winter of 1998, Farrah Fawcett, America's iconic sweetheart, seemed to be losing her mind. She'd been displaying the symptoms of a classic Hollywood celebrity meltdown with a series of erratic and bizarre public appearances. So it was rather surprising in February of that year to receive an invitation to join Farrah and Robert Duvall at a very private screening of *The Apostle*, a film in which both were starring. I remember going to the screener that Sunday evening in February at the Universal Screening Room in New York City and even by 8 p.m. that night—as the likes of Matt Damon, Val Kilmer, Christopher Walken, Naomi Campbell, Michael Stipe, Billy Bob Thornton, Laura Dern, Sheryl Crow, and Ed Harris all made it from the theater to the penthouse for dinner—there was still no sign of Farrah.

The high-end Hollywood wattage had clearly all shown up that evening to see one person and she was nowhere to be found. Then, suddenly, out of seemingly thin air, the very thin image of a woman swathed in a sparkly beige dress appeared. Farrah Fawcett had finally arrived, three hours later than scheduled. She was charming, reed thin, and shaking like a leaf. And the flute of champagne never left her right hand for the entire night. Her dress, she would later tell me, was from the design house of Krizia. Farrah flitted all over the room that night. She never paused in one place for too long for anyone to approach and attempt to have a proper conversation. She was very attentive to her young son Redmond who she had dragged along to this late-night revelry.

As one would expect, that image of Farrah stayed in my mind. Even almost two years after, when I sat to interview yet another Hollywood legend for *Vanity Fair*. . . .

GW: Has it become more difficult for you to deal with the attention of late? Especially the last four years, which have not been the greatest?

FF: I think, looking back at it now, it was more difficult than I had allowed myself to feel. One thing that helped me, that I learned long ago to follow, is that you can't believe everything they write about you, and you can't think that everybody else believes it, or you will be devastated. It's bad enough to have to deal with making your parents uncomfortable with ludicrous things written about you. A long time ago I learned not to place so much importance on the bad—it causes you not to place much importance on the good.

GW: So you would say that your behavior has not been strange at all?

FF: No, I wouldn't say that, but my press has been stranger. I think I always act a little strange. I am more outspoken. I think I take a lot of risks. But do I think my behavior is bizarre, extreme, or strange to the point of harming myself or others? Absolutely not.

GW: What's your relationship with your family? Your parents in Texas can't help but read the stories about Farrah being a druggie.

FF: Sometimes they get a call, and my father will pick up the phone, and they'll say, "Did you know that your daughter has gone to rehab?" And my dad would say no. And they'd say, "Yes, she had to be admitted because she tried to slit her wrists." And the thing is, I would be standing next to him. I've never been in drug rehab!

GW: Have you ever done drugs?

FF: No. I am not a druggie. When I hear stories that I have been sitting in a parking lot doing crack cocaine—I don't even know what crack cocaine is. I don't even know what methamphetamines is. I wouldn't know heroin if I saw it. I know what cocaine looks like, and I certainly know what marijuana is, but I don't even know what Ecstasy is.

GW: What is the acting role you are most proud of to date?

FF: I want to say *The Burning Bed*, because it was such a turning point in my life. Before that it was very difficult for me to get serious roles. I was sort of boxed in by my looks and previous choices and roles.

GW: The role for which you will be most remembered is as Jill Munroe on *Charlie's Angels*. You were only on the show for one year, but of all Charlie's Angels, Farrah is still the one.

FF: That's right, everyone says that. I don't know if it was because that was around the time my poster came out, and there was such an impact with the poster. And then there was my hair, and that affected so much culturally.

GW: That red bathing suit—did you know that one website called it "the poster that stained a thousand sheets"?

FF: I remember when I was first asked that question about that poster—"You know how many people have masturbated to that?" And I went, "No, it never occurred to me."

GW: Where is that red bathing suit?

FF: It's here. My assistant found it in the attic when I had to move because the earthquake destroyed my house. We've been talking to the Smithsonian, and they asked the very same question because they want it.

GW: Surely one of your greatest achievements is becoming a mother at thirty-seven. What is your relationship with Ryan O'Neal, your son's father?

FF: With Ryan it has come to a very good place, where we are able to realize the importance of what we did, have been, and are.

GW: I'm sure Lee Majors will never forgive himself for introducing you to Ryan.

FF: Oh, I don't know, he may be happy he did.

GW: What about that infamous appearance on David Letterman?

FF: I was talking about that the other day, because I am going to be on in October again.

GW: You mean you are going back for more of that torture?

FF: I don't find it torture. The only thing I was really guilty of was being extremely fatigued. I was trying to be a bit silly. I think what I am guilty of is maybe being a bad talk-show guest.

GW: Thank you, Farrah. Stay fabulous.

{ FRANCESCO SCAVULLO }

OCTOBER 1997

In July of 1997 I sat with the great Francesco Scavullo. The legendary fashion and celebrity photographer. Now, looking back on this moment with Scavullo, I think I never did delve as much as I ought to have. I should have probed more about what it was like that day on the set when he photographed the macho icon Burt Reynolds nude, at the request of Helen Gurley Brown and *Cosmopolitan*. That nude spread caused an incredible sensation, as most any photo shoot with Scavullo did back in his heyday. From the 1970s through the 1990s and well after his death in 2004, Scavullo was still an icon of photography. And the man responsible for the careers of Brooke Shields, Cheryl Tiegs, Iman, and, most of all, Farrah Fawcett.

GW: What does the O in Scavullo stand for?

FS: I don't know.

GW: I think it stands for "ordinary."

FS: I don't think I'm ordinary. I don't like ordinary things. I like simple, but not ordinary. I love beautiful women, and I love beautiful men. I've never wanted to destroy beauty. I've always just wanted to make it more beautiful.

GW: I know you've had a few nervous breakdowns, Francesco, but please don't have a fifth one before we get through our little chat.

FS: I don't have any, not anymore. Now I only have mini ones.

GW: Scavullo once said he knew in high school that he wanted to be a photographer. And you had your first magazine contract [at *Seventeen*] as a teenager. Did you ever look back and say, Gee, maybe I was a prodigy?

FS: Well, no, I just thought I was lucky. I was working for Horst.

GW: And by now you have photographed them all, from Liz to Liza to every supermodel. But didn't you have a famous feud with Raquel Welch?

FS: [Muttering] I get on really well with Raquel Welch, but she is difficult. She wants the best out of herself. What usually happens with Raquel is she starts crying, and I put my arms around her and tell her everything is going to be fine. And then we go put the clothes on her and we go to work.

GW: GW's favorite Scavullo classic is that portrait of Diana Ross "unplugged": simple hair, little makeup, T-shirt, and jeans. It was radical for the time.

FS: Diana Ross said she wanted a new look. And the only thing new we could do with Diana Ross was get rid of all the hair. Get rid of the makeup. I wanted to see her like the little urchin. I wanted to see her back to what she was before she added everything. So she came here, we threw on a pair of [the late supermodel] Gia's old jeans, and went to work. Once she saw the pictures, she didn't like them really. Then she showed them to Cher. Cher said, "Girl, you've never looked so good," and then it became Diana Ross's favorite picture.

GW: Scavullo and Brooke Shields are forever linked.

FS: I met Brooke when she was seven months old. Everybody knows that story. I was doing an Ivory soap commercial and all the babies were crying, and Nan Bush, my assistant at the time, said she had this hairdresser friend across the street with the most beautiful baby. I said, "Call her up immediately!" So, in comes Brooke Shields in her mother's arms, and she loved the camera. Even at seven months.

GW: There is a faction of fashion that pooh-poohs Scavullo, irrational snobs who call him a minor talent. In other words, he's no Richard Avedon!

FS: [Long pause.] That I'm no Avedon? Certainly not! I'm Scavullo! I have been working for fifty years. And I've had a wonderful career, a wonderful time being a photographer. And I have a book coming out [*Scavullo: Photographs, 50 Years*] which highlights the fifty years of my photography! I have a style which I have

developed, and I'm not going to change it every fifteen minutes!

GW: Congratulations are in order, Mr. Scavullo! I think
the one thing you still have to do is direct a music
video.

FS: Thank you. But you know I directed Crystal Gayle's
first album special for CBS. But these videos are too
quick. I did think about directing films. I was very
good friends with Luchino Visconti. And he once said
to me "If you really want to direct movies, come to
Europe and be an assistant director on my next film."
I would have had to take a year off, and I thought
about it. But then I said, "If I took a year off, no one
would remember me when I got back to New York,
and this studio would be useless."

LeRoy
Neiman

$\Big\{$ LEROY NEIMAN $\Big\}$

AUGUST 1996

T his great American artist is yet another fine example of GW going to do an interview and ending up becoming very close friends from that day on for the many, many years that followed. LeRoy Neiman was a dear mentor and friend, and I miss him to this day. I always loved his art and more so his innate and unique personal style—and that famous Dalí-like mustache, which he pulled off with the most debonair air. I went to his vast studio on the Upper West Side in the summer of 1998 for the very first time, and as GW is wont to say—there would be many, many more impromptu visits.

GW: You just gifted Columbia University with six million dollars to their School of the Arts. Why?

LN: Columbia's art department should be the strongest, and it's going to be. Columbia is New York, where the biggest art business is. Why shouldn't it have the greatest art department.

GW: And part of it will be the LeRoy Neiman Center for Print Studies. That has a nice ring to it.

LN: Right there in the center of campus.

GW: How did you get this long-running gig as the unofficial artist of the Olympics?

LN: Roone Arledge lived across the street from me, and asked me to. The first [time] was in 1972.

GW: That had to have been something. The 1972 Olympics, the Munich massacre . . .

LN: Yeah . . . I was there, with Jim McKay and all those people. We were all staying at the Sheraton near the Olympic Village. At that time, there was no security. Anybody could walk into the Olympic Village and hang out. One morning at around five, we got a call that there was a disturbance in the Village. We took my car and went over there. We saw the whole thing—we stayed for hours and hours. Some of the victims were on the Israeli wrestling team, too, whom I had just drawn a couple of days before at the opening day march.

GW: You've known Hugh Hefner for many, many years . . .

LN: From before the magazine. At this stage in my life, he's one of my oldest friends, actually. We met because I was doing women's fashion drawings for this milliner in Chicago. Hef was a copywriter in the men's store, and he was doing a cartoon book. He did all the drawings, all the captions, and he got it published. I knew there was something special there. There was a mood going in Chicago, of skin magazines. But they were all trashy, with third-rate advertising. And we met on the street one day, and he had started this magazine, with quality advertising, and Marilyn Monroe was on the cover. I illustrated a story about jazz and won the Chicago Art Directors Club Award.

GW: Did you ever go to any of the orgies at the Playboy Mansion?

LN: My God! Those were firsts for everybody, new experiences for everyone involved. I used to carry a tape measure. And every girl I'd see I would measure, to see if she was the perfect 34-26-34. But we could never do this today.

GW: Weren't you also there when Marilyn Monroe sang "Happy Birthday" to J.F.K. at Madison Square Garden?

LN: I did a painting, and it is in Madison Square Garden. I got Marilyn singing in there, carrying the birthday cake in. I got Adlai Stevenson, L.B.J., Bobby—the whole gang. It was a sensational affair. At that time, to accept a commission to paint some of those events was considered bad taste.

GW: Why is it that art snobs so disdain LeRoy Neiman?

LN: I've never tried to analyze it, but I'd like to say they're coming around. All the things that I've been taken to task for over the years: *Playboy* and my identification with them, television art, which is another form of making money; silkscreens, where I made tons of money—everything that I touched has clicked.

Things that they took me to task for are now what they want the artist to do.

GW: You've been around the world many times over. You've met everyone of consequence. What else is there left for LeRoy Neiman to do?

LN: It's always new. Thirty years ago people walked differently, they moved differently, they looked different. They're human beings. You never have to worry about seeing too much of the world, because it just keeps renewing itself.

{ ANNA WINTOUR }

NOVEMBER 1997

T his is probably still the only Q&A in history that the enigmatic, and newly anointed Dame Anna Wintour, has ever sat for. She actually did this GW Q&A for my Xeroxed, avant-garde style journal called *R.O.M.E.*, of which she was a huge, influential fan. We met her in her *Vogue* office while the headquarters of Condé Nast was still at Madison Avenue. To this day I do believe it is the only interview for which Anna Wintour has ever answered pointed questions on any particular subject, including her then marriage. This GW Q&A is thus one for the record books!

I think Anna was won over by the personal note I wrote, which I still have to this day and which reads as follows:

"Anna Wintour's complexity is always revered, and so it was such the evening's thrill to be in your presence again at Oscar de la Renta's bacchanal the other evening. But the reason for this particular correspondence dearest Anna, is to broach the possibility of GW having a quick audience with the legendary Editrix for the *R.O.M.E.* Volume XXI which debuts in November of 1997. We already have the title—'Anna Speaks!' A quick audience to chat and record the day would be so appreciated. . . ."

Sure enough a few days later that September our dreams were realized. . . .

GW: When people think of Anna Wintour, they think of this cold, aloof fashion editrix. Who is the real Anna Wintour?

AW: Oh, George, that's for you to say. Come on!

GW: Oh no, it's for you to tell me if that's true or not. Do you like that image? Do you care?

AW: No, it's certainly not an image that I cultivate. I think maybe it was printed in one paper and, you know, some journalists just go out and write what they've read somewhere else. I know what the people that I work with think about me, and what my family thinks about me. I don't worry about it.

GW: Tell me a little about your childhood. Was it privileged?

AW: Privileged? Not particularly. My father was an editor of a British newspaper, and my mother worked, but stopped when she had kids. There were four of us.

GW: Where were you in the lineage?

AW: I was second. My childhood was kind of normal.

GW: Did you think, growing up, that you'd one day be one of the most important fashion editors in the world?

AW: Well, I always wanted to get into journalism, I guess because of my father, because he was so known in the newspaper business in England. I guess I chose to go into magazines because that wasn't so much his world. I certainly grew up knowing that being in publishing was something I wanted to do.

GW: What is a typical day in the life of Anna Wintour?

AW: I'll tell you what I did today. I got up at six, I read some copy, talked to my husband, got my kids up, made them breakfast, took them to school . . .

GW: You take them to school yourself?

AW: Every morning, yes. I took them to school, I had a nine a.m. meeting with about ten people about a trip being planned to Russia, then I read some more copy, edited, had a features meeting, then went to Seventh Avenue and had a fitting with Geoffrey Beene. Then I went to Marc Jacobs [at Perry Ellis], had lunch with him, and he showed me what he's thinking about for his fall collection. And then I came back here. I looked at some pictures in the art department. I had a run-through with Carlyne Cerf, and now I'm here with you.

GW: Do you meet with fashion designers a lot?

AW: I do. I try and get into the market. I find it very helpful. Every time you go out there you get an idea; you get something that is in some way going to be translated back into the magazine. Some [of the designers] are more accessible and easier than others, but it's fun. I love being in the market.

GW: Are you happy with your current state of American fashion?

AW: [Laughs] I found the spring collections very, very interesting. I thought there was an enormous amount of ideas there. There is an awful lot of choice. Obviously there's kind of a sixties thing going on, which I think is great. What I thought was particularly strong was the amount of choice.

GW: One thing I find especially appealing about you is the incongruous nature of your marriage. Your husband is a psychiatrist. He is not a particularly stylish man. He seems to be everything Anna Wintour is not. Tell me a little thing about your husband, your courting. How long have you been married?

AW: We've been married six years, five or six years, I can never remember. I met him through English friends about seven years ago. His first wife was actually a fashion designer, so I guess he likes fashion. After he was separated from his wife, I was reintroduced to him.

GW: So it was a quick romance?

AW: Pretty quick, pretty quick.

GW: What do you think about *Mirabella* magazine?

AW: [Pause] Well . . . to me, it's not a fashion magazine. I think it's heavier on the features. It seems to be a more general interest magazine, and obviously, to my eye, it seems aimed at an older reader than some of the other magazines of that kind. I think its size is great. I wish I could have that size.

GW: Do you read it?

AW: No, I don't. That has nothing to do with *Mirabella* because I really don't read any other magazines.

GW: You don't read other magazines?

AW: Not in the fashion world. So many other people are obsessed with what other people are doing. I take a quick look, but there's too much out there. For my own personal reading, I'd rather read the *New York Times* or *R.O.M.E.*, something that's not so much my world and my point of view. I don't want to be influenced by what other people may be doing.

GW: Do you read *Vanity Fair*?

AW: Well, I certainly look at *Vanity Fair* and sometimes read it on the plane. But again, it's just really a question of time. My weekends I usually read a book. *Vanity Fair* is a terrific magazine, but I'm not poring over it to see what they are doing.

GW: What do you think of Tina Brown?

AW: A brilliant editor.

GW: Is she a friend?

AW: Yes, I've known Tina for a long time, and her husband is a great, great friend of my father's. And I have great respect for Tina. I think she's doing an amazing job.

GW: Would you say that *Vogue* under your tutelage has incorporated a "downtown sensibility"?

AW: [Laughs] I don't think we edit with uptown or downtown in mind. I think we edit for a woman that's interested in fashion. It's a personal attitude, I think. Maybe there is a bit of downtown, maybe there's a bit of L.A. It's a mix, more than one point of view.

GW: If there is one thing you would change about your physical appearance, what would it be?

AW: I'd be taller. I think I'd like to be taller.

GW: Not a longer neck?

AW: Just more height.

GW: Do you aspire to do anything more than this job?

AW: Well, you never know what's going to happen, but this is such a great job, and I'm having so much fun. I certainly want to be here for the foreseeable future.

{ CINDY ADAMS }

FEBRUARY 2003

Cindy, you know GW adores you. But when are you going to clatter off into the sunset with your pen and stilettos?

If ever there was my "claim to fame"—ridiculous as it may sound—it was on the set of a photo shoot at the behest of *New York* magazine. It was an all-day shoot at the Plaza Hotel, all devised by a then *New York* magazine genius of an editor by the name of Maer Roshan. It was his idea to stage this photo shoot between GW and CA and to then—for the record—record the totally unscripted, multi-page badinage between us that ensued after the shoot. That unforgettable magazine article that ran with the banner headline "Gossip Queens" remains to this day one of the most crème-de-la-crème moments of this ink-stained wretch's blessed existence. I will never forget, ever, that photo shoot with Cindy Adams as we preened and gleamed for the cameras that day at the revered Plaza Hotel.

I reveled in the moment. And could you blame me? This is a woman who, from what I understand, has been a friend and confidante of seemingly every famous man and woman on the planet. Cindy Adams has known them all and can recall a personal anecdote of every famous person, living and dead. So the fact that she was seemingly purring so breathlessly made me happy that Cindy was so comfortable and enjoying the moment. I certainly did. Still love you, Cindy Adams!

GW: Cindy Adams was born circa what, 1900? She still looks fabulous, even though she is from the brontosaurus era.

CA: You're so good at what you do. You're so good. Does anyone get ticked?

GW: Once in a while, but my audience knows this is all in jest. Cindy, you've gone to the dogs. You've written a book about your dog, Jazzy. Or is it really your memoirs?

CA: There is a little bit of memoir in it, George, but I wasn't looking to write my memoirs, because I don't believe in memoirs from people like me. And then I saw Clint Eastwood—

GW: Do you have to start name-dropping already, Cindy?

CA: Well, I just don't think anyone wants to read a book about me. What happened was very simple: Joey was with me for about a thousand years, and when he left I was talking one night with a publisher friend of mine, and he thought that I should have someone in my life, so he gave me a Yorkie. And he sent him in by limo. So the story is about what it is like to be a dog who lives with the gossip columnist.

GW: How are you managing without Joey—living in this big old apartment by yourself?

CA: He was all I had, George.

GW: You probably have more servants than Prince Charles, so I'm sure you are never alone. So Miss Bagel is doing fine.

CA: You bitch! You can never get classy in your old age, no way, with people like you. I'm okay. I've surrounded myself with friends.

GW: How is it that you and Joey never had any children?

CA: Joey was fairly senior when we got married and he didn't want to have any kids. It would be nice. But you know, Jazzy's getting a boutique in his name at Macy's. "Jazzy of Park Avenue," they're calling it— collars, leashes, bowls, mugs . . . a very New York thing.

GW: I hope your book will sell much better than your gossip fragrance.

CA: I know that I smelled almost as bad as some of the stuff I write. Thank you very much, you bastard.

GW: Tell me about Liza Minnelli's wedding to David Gest. You were there.

CA: It was "Eighteenth Century Fox," I'm telling you. The bridesmaids came out of the crypt. I was the junior member—what can I tell you? Marisa Berenson looked gorgeous. Liz Taylor didn't seem to know where she was, and she forgot her shoes. They carried her in on this sedan chair and plopped her down, and she had her feet in these furry bunny slippers. And then there was Janet Leigh, who kept asking for Vaseline. If she smiled her lips would crack. The whole thing was so bizarre.

GW: What about hagarella Imelda?

CA: Imelda can only come here with permission. The Philippine government is very tough on her because she mislaid something like half a billion dollars. She seems to have forgotten where she put it. Every once in a while she's allowed to leave. All my great friends are in the can. Manuel Noriega, Imelda . . .

GW: My favorite Cindy Adams–Imelda story took place in the Waldorf Towers.

CA: That's a true story. I was with Imelda, and she turned her living room into a church. She made an altar out of a coffee table. And a priest was ready to do Mass, and all of a sudden she turned to me and said, "I have to hide you. Doris Duke is coming up. She's going to bring me five million dollars in bail." I saw her come in with two lawyers, just before they locked me in the toilet.

GW: And the kicker is that you are now living in Doris Duke's apartment. How funny. You're such a strong woman, Cindy. Thank you so much.

Martha
Stewart

The first time I ever set eyes on Martha Stewart was on September 17, 1993, at the JFK International Airport. We were part of a motley crew of pioneers who were invited to visit Moscow for a week and to attend the very grand opening of the first Western-style nightclub Moscow had ever seen. As I said—it was a historic moment! Boris Yeltsin was running the Kremlin and swilling a lot of vodka along the way, as our bemused host would later tell us over one of many, many sumptuous Russian banquets served up to the Manhattan visitors. Amongst the crew that gathered giddily by the Delta/Aeroflot gate to take part in this unforgettable experience were the likes of the gonzo journo from "Page Six," Richard Johnson, and other pop critics, such as the foodie Gael Greene, the hip hotelier André Balazs, and the fashion maven Fern Mallis. As I arrived at the gate at precisely 6:15 p.m. that night, Martha Stewart,

I distinctly remember, was being interviewed right there by the CBS cameras of Connie Chung and her then TV show called *Eye to Eye*. Suffice it to say, being asked to be part of this New York gaggle gracing Moscow with its presence, and being wined and dined and, yes, sixty-nined—I was, anyway, by the end of this, my first of two unforgettable visits to Moscow—back to Martha . . . I finally interviewed Martha Stewart almost a year later in 1994, when we had lunch at the hallowed restaurant the Four Seasons. I remember showing up for lunch jacketless and being tossed a fusty, old, ill-fitting jacket by owner Julian Niccolini before being allowed to sit with Martha. And when we did sit to speak, all Martha Stewart had for lunch that day was a Four Seasons baked potato!

GW: Don't think for one minute that because we're having lunch at the Four Seasons this interview is going to be all kissy-kissy, Martha.

MS: Oh gosh, you're starting already. I don't frighten that easily. You can't intimidate me on my turf.

GW: I'm still a little peeved at you, actually. I saw you being chauffeured off alone one night from this soirée in Central Park. And I shouted, "Martha!" You whipped that WASPy head around, saw this Negro waving to you, and whipped back around.

MS: I'm not a WASP—I'm a Polish-American. I'm the daughter of Polish immigrants and I'm Catholic. I'm not WASPy. I am tall and blond. I have my beautiful Polish heritage to thank for that.

GW: Are you a real blonde or a bottle blonde?

MS: I'm a real blonde.

GW: Who would have thought your magazine, *Martha Stewart Living*, would evolve into such an overwhelming success! But I have only one problem with it. Do you have to be on the cover of every issue?

MS: I'm not—on the current issue it's my roses. I really have a hard time posing, but our readers really like it.

GW: You mean it flies off the shelf when you're on the cover?

MS: Oh gosh yes, but it also flies off the shelf when I'm not on the cover.

GW: I don't have a problem with you on the cover, but not on every issue, Ma-a-artha!

MS: We are establishing a brand, and we want to make sure that it's very secure before we start tampering with it. So this year there are three issues without me out of eight, so that's pretty good.

GW: Do you ever show signs of humility?

MS: I am not an un-humble person. I still clean up the kitty litter, and the chicken coop. And I still garden and wash the floors if they have to be washed.

GW: Do you scrub your own bathtub?

MS: You bet I do. But in my business I try very hard not to create a hierarchy. We have titles, but the hierarchical kind of approach is not really for me. If I have a housekeeper, I want that housekeeper to think that she is the most important director of my television series, and she is.

187

GW: You know so much about weddings. How come you don't have a husband?

MS: I had a husband. I had a very nice husband. But he became not so nice.

GW: What happened?

MS: I can't figure it out, George. He wanted the divorce, not I.

GW: Well, he must be getting a lot of palimony. I read once where you only need four hours' sleep. It certainly doesn't show. Do you use a lot of Chanel night cream?

MS: Mario Badescu Revitalin Night Cream, that's what I use.

GW: Some people consider you a superwoman.

MS: How nice—I'd love to be thought of as that.

GW: And what do you do for kicks? You climb Mount Kilimanjaro!

MS: That was actually really interesting. That was last October. I don't want to endanger myself, but I do want adventure.

GW: I hate how perfect you are. Give me a proclamation about lifestyle in the nineties.

MS: In the nineties, we are seeing greater attention to detail and quality. We're not looking for instant gratification anymore, but we are still looking for a lifestyle that has elegance and curiosity.

{ HELEN GURLEY BROWN }

JUNE 2000

HGB was at her desk that Manhattan summer afternoon. A glamorous, perfectly coiffed, wrinkled wraith who nonetheless was still a fabulous sight to behold. And I could never forget—minutes after I took up her offer of the chair across from her desk, she couldn't stop gushing about how much she enjoyed the exclusive *VF* photo shoot. And who could blame the woman who defined "cougar" before the term even existed? Helen Gurley Brown's photo of her being hoisted by the most gorgeous Chippendale's-like blond studmuffin is an early twenty-first-century photo classic buried somewhere in those *VF* archives. She was as giddy as a schoolgirl coquettishly kicking up her stilettos. I spent ninety minutes with the magazine industry icon, and it was quite a ride!

GW: Your book's title threw GW. He kept thinking, When was this old broad not wild?

HGB: The truth is I've just been writing for six years. And I said to my husband, "This is just a collection of snippets, thoughts, philosophies, anguishes, happinesses— just snippets from my life." And he said, "You're crazy. You can't call that book Snippets From My Life—nobody will go near it. Here's a title for you: I'm Wild Again." And I thought it was something legitimate. It means I'm writing again. And it means every time I write I say something outrageous, and now is no exception.

GW: First and foremost, what are Helen Gurley Brown's thoughts on vaginal plastic surgery?

HGB: On what?

GW: Vaginal cosmetic surgery. Is it a trend for the twenty-first century?

HGB: I am not knowledgeable—not whatsoever. I have heard of a vagina being made smaller, tighter. That has been around for quite a while.

GW: What about enhancing the labia? The vaginal lips?

HGB: I'm not knowledgeable about it. But it seems like absolute insanity to me, to do these extra little things. I don't think you can make an orgasm any better. An orgasm is an orgasm. You do it, you climax—wonderful, terrific!

GW: But a lot of women don't have orgasms.

HGB: Well, if this particular kind of procedure is supposed to help them, I suppose I could be informed about it. But I'm pretty passionate about the idea that your brain gives you orgasms, along with your cooperating body.

GW: Is David Brown, your husband, on Viagra?

HGB: That's very personal! I would go so far as to say that David is doing fine without Viagra.

GW: Are you upset? Is that too personal?

HGB: Whatever I have said, I have said.

GW: You had sex with Jack Dempsey. Was he the best—

HGB: No, he was fine. I wouldn't like to get into the specifics.

GW: C'mon, girl!

HGB: That would be denigrating to my husband, who is pretty good. I don't want to be out there saying such.

GW: Your *Cosmopolitan* took off from the first hour.

HGB: Yes, it was an instant success.

GW: And you've said that Rex Harrison is the rudest celebrity you've ever met in your life.

HGB: I guess so—he was really quite abusive. I don't remember bad celebrities, because I tend to respect them and not take advantage of them. Sharon Stone may have given me a bit of a problem. We did a cover shoot, which was a really big deal because we rarely did celebrities at *Cosmo*. We did the Cindy Crawfords and Rene Russos of the world, the gorgeous professional models of the time. So to do a movie star was a big deal. We did Sharon and we gave her photo approval, which we rarely did. When she saw the pictures, she didn't like any of them. It wasn't an attack on me personally, but it was time and money. And we had to start over because she didn't think the picture was okay.

GW: Was it hard for you to give it all up? Did they have to push you out the door?

HGB: They did not have to push me out the door. And I wouldn't even say it was tough to give up the actual job. It's a big challenge to put out a successful magazine every twenty-eight working days. And after having done it for thirty-two years and at seventy-five years old, I wasn't devastated, but I still miss the power. You are very influential as a magazine editor. Everybody courts you and adores you and makes a big fuss over you—and all the free stuff, all the baskets of cosmetics and the closets of clothes. I miss the power and the perks. But people still come up to me on the street and tell me "You've changed my life." This new assignment as editor in chief of International Editions means I have gone to twenty-four different countries to start new *Cosmos*. I just got back from Spain, where they have started a twenty-four-hour *Cosmo* TV station. And next I'm going to Athens to launch *Cosmo* to Greece. So I'm busy.

Fabio

$$\left\{\text{FABIO}\right\}$$

NOVEMBER 1992

I t all began with Fabio in November of 1992, when my favorite "Vanities" [in *Vanity Fair*] editor of them all, Matthew Tyrnauer, called to tell me the news that Graydon Carter had green-lit the GW Q&A column and that my first celebrity interview would be with the kitschy romance cover hunk by the name of Fabio. At the time, his publicist hacks were dubbing him "America's Romance Ambassador," and the reason for this auspicious debut was the fact that he was releasing his first pinup or "sensuous" calendar. Needless to say, GW and Fabio hit it off from the get-go, and despite his mangled Milanese version of English, the interview went very well.

GW: Why are you so different from any other brawny, blond, blue-eyed hunk?

F: Maybe it's because I'm humble. I don't come across as cocky, or full of myself, I guess.

GW: How much time do you spend in front of the mirror each morning?

F: Not very much. I go in, take a shower, brush my teeth, blow-dry my hair, and then I'm out.

GW: Your image is on the cover of more than 350 Avon romance novels. You've sold many a trashy love story dressed as a Viking, pirate, prince, etc. Now Avon has given you a six-figure contract to write three books, and you have never written a day in your life! Some women novelists are upset at your getting this deal.

F: True. But I have great fantasies, and that's what women want—fantasy. Most of the women writers are happy for me getting this deal. There are only five or six writers who are upset. All the big writers in the business are on my side.

GW: You have a number, 1-900-90FABIO, where women can call to talk to you. What do you talk about?

F: I talk about the differences between men and women, and ways to improve communication between the sexes.

GW: I understand, however, that you don't have a girl-friend. Do you have a boyfriend?

F: [Laughs] No. I love women. I'm sorry. I adore women. For me, women are the best thing God ever put on earth.

GW: Does Fabio mean fabulous in Italian?

F: [Laughs] No. But in America it does.

GW: How big are your arms?

F: About eighteen inches [around].

GW: What about the third arm?

F: [Laughs] It's in proportion to everything else.

GW: My God, it must be humongous! You also have the most enormous breasts I've ever seen on any man. How long have you been working out?

F: Since I was sixteen. I started working out after I broke my leg skiing. I was a competitive skier from when I was five. When I broke my left leg, I went to the gym for rehabilitation; that's how I got into working out.

GW: You have so many physical assets. What is your least favorite?

F: I'm happy with myself . . .

GW: That's easy for you to say.

F: I think everybody should be happy with themselves. I appreciate every single thing God gave me. It is important to love yourself and to love other people.

GW: You say you are negotiating to do another TV pilot for CBS, but would you consider doing a soft-porn movie?

F: No, never.

GW: What if the co-star were Sharon Stone?

F: Well, if it's a film like *Basic Instinct*, maybe. I don't believe that in order to act you have to show intimate parts of your body.

GW: Lately, you've been peddling your very own pinup calendar.

F: I'm very proud of my calendar. I'm the first man to

ever have his own calendar. My calendar sells more than Cindy Crawford's or Claudia Schiffer's.

GW: Oh, let's not talk about her.

F: My calendar sold two hundred thousand copies in one month. They can't keep it on the shelves; it's already in its sixth printing. In December, I'm going to be signing my calendar in Beverly Hills.

GW: Yeah, but I wanted to see you in a G-string, and your calendar doesn't show that.

F: Well, you'll have to wait to buy the 1994 calendar.

{ SARAH FERGUSON }
—*Duchess of York*

MAY 2000

T his is one of the very first interviews that the Duchess of York gave to any journalist living in the United States, and she insisted on meeting me in person. So I flew to Richmond, Virginia, to sit before her in Suite 252 of the vast and dowdy Jefferson Hotel. At the time, in the year 2000, "Fergie" wasn't so much the media-savvy press maven she would become after having to retreat from a serious series of malodorous scandals that almost sullied her brand into oblivion. Back then she was very much still the true blue-blooded British royal, on this trip to Virginia with Buckingham Palace footing the bill for her and her entourage of royal advisers. And so we settled in the anteroom of her suite at this dowager Virginia hotel to speak. This interview was conducted before Fergie's toe-sucking scandal.

I had the great pleasure of being again in the company of

Sarah Ferguson, a full ten years after we first met, when out of the blue I got an invitation from the Duchess of York to join her for tea at the Mandarin Hotel. Wow! She was definitely not as fabulously groomed as the first time I met her in that dowdy, old-money Virginia hotel. But I didn't care because Fergie was so much fun that day. So it was such a shock when—it couldn't have been but a few days later—I picked up the *Daily Mail* of May 23, 2010, and read that Fergie was essentially being called "the greedy black sheep" of the Royal Family, and saw those embarrassing photos of her counting ill-gotten gains. I felt bad for her because she really means well and has such an incredible spirit.

GW will always adore Sarah Ferguson. And this is our GW Q&A from back in 2000.

GW: The amazing thing about the Duchess's Weight Watchers gig is that, unlike the other celebrity-diet phenomena, you have managed to keep it off. Just look at those gams on the Duchess of York! Are the legs insured by Lloyd's of London?

SF: I've thought about that.

GW: Tell me, do you still consider yourself part of the royal family?

SF: No. I see myself as a very natural mother interested in all sides of life. I'm definitely not part of the royal family. I am very pleased I can give my girls the balance they need to go forward. Because they have to know that life is tough, that ten families in Kosovo live under one roof.

GW: Has it reached the point at all where Beatrice will look at you and say, "Mummy, why does Grandpa hate you so much?"

SF: Oh, yes. I don't know if she's ever used the word "hate." But I think they both want to know why I am excluded from the royal family and family engagements. And I have to explain to them, "That's just the way it is, and you know what your mummy is like. And you know she has been misrepresented. But that's the way they have chosen to be. But you know, I am slightly different, don't you think, girls?" And the girls say, "Well, Mummy, you're such fun." And I say, "Well, you've got to learn in life that not everybody can like your fun." Which I learnt at forty, and which they can learn at nine.

GW: But certainly it must be the greatest pain for you: the treatment by Prince Philip. Recently I saw a story about him, and its headline was PRINCE OF DARKNESS. Is Prince Philip your Private Enemy Number One?

SF: I don't think of it like that at all. I actually respect him enormously. I think he's very intelligent.

GW: Really? The article said, "His major life's work has been to walk five paces behind his far more important wife."

SF: But that's what's so difficult for this poor man.

GW: And you consider him smart, even though he says that your role is pointless.

SF: I can't change his mind, so I've come to accept it.

GW: When was the last time you saw him face to face?

SF: Halloween.

GW: Halloween? For what, like five seconds?

SF: I took the girls to see Granny and Grandpa, and he said hello, and I said hello. Granny is wonderful, so special.

GW: You are one of the survivors.

SF: Yes, I've kept my head on my shoulders. Usually when you leave the royal family you have your head cut off. They've all been beheaded. When I was in bankruptcy I was offered many jobs in Britain. Volkswagen offered me major money to do a TV ad. I said no, because it would be rubbing the nose at the royal family. I will not betray Her Majesty.

GW: The two tragedies in your life . . .

SF: There've been three: Diana first, then Mum, and then Carolyn Cotterell, who was my best friend in the world. She died last year.

GW: When Diana died, you weren't on speaking terms.

SF: Right. I'm the sort of person that loves unconditionally. Did it matter when she wasn't speaking to me? It did, it killed me, I hated it. But I understood that that was just the way she was. There are times she would go into her shell, and I would understand that. I didn't like it, and I'd always wonder what I'd done wrong to deserve it. She was very clever.

GW: And then that phone call in the middle of the night that your mother had been killed, also in a car accident. Was that the worst moment of your life?

SF: No. FERGIE SHOULD BE EXILED—when they wrote that.

GW: Sarah would love to remarry Prince Andrew. Wouldn't she?

SF: No, marriage is a tough journey. All that stuff is put on the back burner for the moment.

GW: Why do you continue to put yourself through the torture of Christmas alone at Sandringham [the royal family's estate in Norfolk]?

SF: I like it. I spend five days doing whatever I like. I watch my movies, walk my dogs, and I'm really happy. I like being alone, watching old Cary Grant movies. I'm there, I never have to put any makeup on. I get the girls up in the morning, get them dressed; they go up [to the castle to see the royal family]. I have the whole day to myself, and they come back in the evening.

GW: Prince Philip must be fuming.

SF: They're all fuming and doing what they like, but I love it. I light the fire, put on my movies, and I'm happy.

{ RUSSELL SIMMONS }

Having known the hip-hop mogul and visionary from my first arrival in New York City, I was expecting this sit-down with him in the early autumn of 2003 to be a breeze. I did not expect him to insist that I spend the entire day with him. He dragged me from an early morning yoga class to his corner suite at Def Jam Records and then to a local Manhattan radio station where he was having a live call-in with the most notorious urban radio DJ at the time—one Wendy Williams. Yes, the very same virago who helms a very successful syndicated morning talk show on the Fox network. I will never forget sitting in the green room of Hot 97 FM as they gabbed away. Wendy Williams likes to mouth off a lot and it has made her a very wealthy woman.

And she had Russell on his toes, not literally, the entire afternoon. But he was no match for GW.

GW: Were you at Café Tabac the night that Christy Turlington squatted behind the bar?

RS: I don't think I was there that night, but I was there
many nights with Christy Turlington, and we had a
lot of fun. Back then we all drank so much, and she
would drink you under the table and be stone-faced,
smiling in her Chanel suit.

GW: It's hard to imagine that Russell Simmons used to sell
ganja on 205th Street in Queens.

RS: Really?

GW: According to your book. Or is that just tweaked autobiography to add street credibility?

RS: I did sell fake cocaine.

GW: It's even harder to imagine that you were addicted not
to marijuana, not to cocaine or crack, but to angel
dust! When did you become sober?

RS: When I turned thirty.

GW: And you are not the first person to say that yoga has
changed his life.

RS: I started practicing yoga religiously eight years ago.

GW: Who was the first rap artiste discovered by Russell
Simmons?

RS: Kurtis Blow, whose first single was "Christmas Rap-
pin'," in 1979.

GW: You founded Def Jam in 1984. What gave you the
balls to think you could start your own record company?

RS: Rick Rubin—who was a member of the Beastie Boys,

who I was managing at the time—had this logo, Def Jam, and since I had so much success managing Run-DMC and Kurtis Blow and Whodini and other rappers, Rick said we should start a label.

GW: Many inductees into the Hip Hop Hall of Fame will come from the label Def Jam—Run-DMC, the Beastie Boys—but as far as GW is concerned, your greatest discovery is LL Cool J.

RS: That's my man. We just re-signed LL Cool J—still with us after twenty years.

GW: Def Jam has made about three hundred million dollars in 2003 so far. How much of that money goes into your pocket?

RS: I'm now just the chairman of Def Jam, and they send a little.

GW: A few million?

RS: That company is owned by Vivendi. Now I only get a bonus. I've discovered that being attached to money is a source of anxiety. It doesn't mean anything.

GW: One of the quirks of your marriage [to Kimora Lee Simmons] is that you and your wife keep separate fridges.

RS: That's because I am vegan and she is not. My refrigerator is vegan and hers is not.

GW: Do you also have separate bedrooms?

RS: No, we sleep together.

GW: What about living in the biggest private residence on the East Coast in Saddle River, New Jersey?

RS: That's not true at all. It is absolutely not the biggest private residence on the East Coast. It is certainly an excellent, beautiful, well-designed home.

GW: Tell GW, do you really think we need a Russell Simmons energy drink? This just sounds like someone's ego run amok.

RS: It's flying off the shelves, blowing out the stores. And a big piece of that profit goes to funding the Hip Hop Summit [a Simmons project that uses hip-hop stars to promote political and social reform], so we really do need it. It is necessary; it's about endowment. It's the healthiest of all energy drinks. It contains no ephedra, like the other energy drinks.

GW: You run a fashion company, Russell, but your personal style leaves a lot to be desired. Russell Simmons is a perfect candidate for *Queer Eye for the Straight Guy.*

RS: Get outta here! What are you talking about, man? I'm wearing the best sportswear in the world—Phat Farm. I'm always fly. My sportswear is always just right and up to date. I disagree.

GW: GW can't help but ponder the notion that somewhere in his cranium Russell Simmons is cradling the idea of one day becoming the first black governor of the great state of New York—say, circa 2020. Seventeen years from now you will be sixty-two years old, the perfect age to mount a gubernatorial campaign.

RS: I don't see that in a million years. I have no political ambitions.

GW: That remains to be seen. Thank you, Mr. Rush.

Eartha Kitt

$\left\{\text{EARTHA KITT}\right\}$

JUNE 2001

E artha Kitt still had it going on. The attitude, the guile, the signature purr, and her indefatigable sensual prowess—all firmly intact even though as she herself said on April 5, 1991, when I saw her for the first time, "two days ago I became 2,500 years old." She was almost seventy, yet there she was perched on a stool, dressed in glittering jewels and a sinuous full-length gown of chain-link shimmer, still holding court in the cabaret at the Carlyle hotel in New York City. Eartha Kitt in her natural wild amongst the posh hoi polloi. Her ruby-red lips were the first thing I noticed as she cooed, "Take me for a walk along the shore of the Bosphorus." The uptown demimonde swooned ever so blithely. "I've had my share, drank my fill, and even though I am satisfied I'm hungry still." Eartha Kitt was simply mesmerizing. After her show her business manager at the time and a dear old friend, Jason Weinberg, took me backstage to meet this fearless, flawless legend. And I was a nervous wreck as I slithered into the aging diva's tiny quarters. Eartha extended her hand, and I obsequiously bowed and quivered. "I owe the people of Turkey a great deal," she purred. "When I decided to sing that song in Turkish, everyone told me that no one would buy it, that it would never sell. Well, where are they today?" I wouldn't have the opportunity to finally interview Eartha Kitt until a full nine years later! Which, come to think of it, looking back, is rather remarkable. It took almost another decade for me to once again meet Eartha Kitt, and she was still fierce and in top form. In December 2000, at the dawn of the twenty-first century, Eartha Kitt was still queen bee, and still doling out anecdotes and advice in a book she was promoting at the time. Her third book, it was aptly subtitled *It's Never Too Late.*

GW: From reading your latest book, *Rejuvenate! (It's Never Too Late)*, it's obvious that Ms. Kitt at seventy-four still maintains a rigorous workout regimen. She is still even able to do somersaults!

EK: Yes, so what are you asking me?

GW: It seems that Ms. Kitt is almost fanatical about her jogging and her stretching.

EK: No, I'm not fanatical about anything. I just believe in keeping myself physically fit.

GW: Eartha Kitt can be haughty; she can be aloof, as cold as ice, and that's when she is being pleasant. She is not an easy person to warm up to.

EK: Yes, because I don't like wallowing in a lot of nonsense, and people meandering up to me because of who I am.

GW: Like it or not, Eartha Kitt will go to her grave being described as a "sex kitten." In your new book, you say, "A great meal can bring on a desire for sex." For Ms. Kitt, a green salad with vinegar-and-olive-oil dressing is enough to make her horny.

EK: It's enough to make you horny if you like what you're eating.

GW: She even considers a baked potato an aphrodisiac.

EK: Did I say that?

GW: Yes.

EK: A baked *sweet* potato.

GW: Isn't it one of your best kept secrets that you had sex with Orson Welles circa 1950?

EK: I never had sex with Orson Welles. I played opposite him in his production of *Dr. Faustus*, as Helen of Troy. It was a working situation and nothing else.

GW: Another interesting revelation from your new book is that you like to walk around your house naked, even outdoors.

EK: Yes, it's true, because I like the fresh air breathing on my body. And I like the feeling of being rejuvenated through the auspices of the gods.

GW: Tell me about January 18, 1968: the White House luncheon you probably wish you had never gone to.

EK: I'm glad I did go to it. I was asked to give my opinions about the problems among the young people at the time, and getting involved with the Vietnam War.

And when I raised my hand and was given the floor by Mrs. Johnson, that is what I told her.

GW: You expressed your opposition to the war, which upset the FBI and CIA, and got you blacklisted for years. Where did you gather the strength and courage to move on, knowing in your heart you didn't do anything wrong?

EK: That I didn't do anything wrong—*that* gave me the strength. Parents still thank me for helping to stop the war.

GW: Do you ever have any regrets for not having a significant other for any lengthy period of time? You were married once, but for only five years.

EK: Once was enough. And I have the most beautiful child from that marriage. So whatever the marriage was like, I was tremendously rewarded for that.

GW: Of your more than thirty albums, which is the definitive Eartha Kitt?

EK: *Eartha Kitt at the Plaza*—that's my favorite.

GW: You've met some remarkable minds in your time, including Albert Einstein.

EK: I was going down a list of orphanages that I give money to. Every year I close my eyes and I go down the line with my finger, and where it stops is the one I give the money to. It happened that that year I wanted to meet Dr. Einstein. Everybody told me it was impossible. But as I was writing the check to this orphanage, I asked if there was anybody there who could introduce me to Dr. Einstein. It so happened that the mistress of the orphanage knew his secretary, and that's how I got to meet him. And I went to see him in Princeton and had tea with him. I think it was December 11, 1954.

GW: And what was your first impression?

EK: It was as if I had known him all my life. We talked about American musical theater and German theater. He was wearing a gray Mickey Mouse T-shirt, and his hair was sticking out as if he had just put his finger in an electric plug. I remember he spoke German to me standing at the top of the stairs—"Why does such a young person want to meet such an old man like me?"

GW: You have said that if someone gave you a diamond you would probably hock it.

EK: I probably would because I like land better. To hold on to material things is an aberration.

{ PRINCE FEDERICO PIGNATELLI } DELLA LEONESSA

Prince Federico Pignatelli della Leonessa is one of the most important icons of the fashion industry. Most fashionistas do not realize that because he is not one to toot his own horn. But trust me when I say that he has been one of the genius visionaries of the business of fashion for twenty years and counting. He is the mastermind behind what I like to refer to as "the Paramount studios of the fashion industry": Pier 59 Studios. It remains the best and largest fashion studio and hub of photography in the world.

Prince Federico Pignatelli della Leonessa will be the first to tell you that since he founded Pier 59 Studios in 1993, "We have housed and hosted more than 50,000 photo shoots. Designers such as Oscar de la Renta, Balmain, Valentino, and Victoria's Secret have created their international fashion campaigns here."

In 2016 he photographed and produced *The Great Beauty*, a gorgeous compilation of his own provocative photography, "to reflect my passion as an admirer and collector of the art of photography," Pignatelli said.

GW: Tell me about this bold, new venture for the Pier 59 brand and the model agency you are creating called Industry Management.

FP: We feel this is a natural progression for Pier 59 Studios. The idea is to now also represent emerging photographers and discovering new model talent and have that element now part of this nexus of talent discovery.

GW: Whenever I meet anyone with truly exemplary and truly exquisite style, I tend to pass that off to good breeding. In this instance, GW could not be more on point.

FP: Yes, it is a fact that my Italian family is quite old and dates back more than eleven hundred years. It is a family that has its root in the southern part of Italy, Naples, Sicily. A family very much connected to the Vatican throughout its history. Yes, one of my ancestors in 1692 became Pope Innocenzo XII. We have also had four cardinals in our family—so, a rich history with the Catholic Church.

GW: How did a descendant of a Pope end up here, ruling New York City?

FP: Ruling New York City?

GW: Well, ruling the whirl of fashion and being a visionary and a maverick.

FP: Well, I cannot say that I am ruling anything, but I try to do my best in being a part of this beautiful world of fashion and creativity in photography. I came to New York City to first pursue a career in investment banking and I left that to develop this Pier 59, which today remains the largest photo studio complex in the world here in New York City, still the capital of photography, creativity, and fashion.

GW: I tell people that you are "the Agnelli of the fashion business"—your incredible style and rakish charm and the fact that you have created what I consider a fashion masterpiece with your Pier 59 Studios. Think of it before you had the vision to develop this part of New York City—west Chelsea was nothing but a run-down, derelict, abandoned part of town. Before there was the chic Meatpacking District, before there was any Chelsea Arts District, Pignatelli came in and resurrected an entire neighborhood.

FP: Well, in fact I knew Gianni Agnelli, aka "The Avocato," who was indeed a very charismatic and wonderful person with an incredible sense of humor and who was indeed extremely Italian and elegant. So that is very much a compliment. Thank you. But, it is all about having a vision and sometimes that vision may be nothing more than intuition. I knew this building, this whole complex had a lot of history. This was the passenger cruise ship terminal in the early days for famous cruise liners crossing the Atlantic. So I decided in 1992 to revive this complex and reinvent it for a new century.

GW: You mentioned the words intuition and instinct, which are two incredible gifts of any true visionary. So here we are twenty years later, Pier 59 Studios is still considered the premier destination for the world's leading photographers, fashion editors, videographers, supermodels, etc.—I was just here recently having lunch with you and was just mesmerized that seemingly every current supermodel in the world was parading back and forth. For Pier 59 to continue to have that sustainability and that longevity is in itself an incredible achievement. And so we must celebrate these twenty-one years of your vision in 2017. Pier 59 Studios is where the magic happens and you ought to be very proud of this achievement.

FP: Well, I feel honored that the important folk of fashion continue to share in this passion of mine. This is a place where I have devoted all my heart into creating a place where photographers and artists of all types can continue to express themselves.

GW: Talk about your fabulous book: *The Great Beauty*.

FP: I had the idea of taking eleven models to the former Italian villa of Paul Getty and creating this book to celebrate the twentieth anniversary of the studio. I wanted that piece of Italy to be part of the celebration. We took an entire crew and spent six days there, thirty-five people in all with the view of creating something special. So the book is my celebration of beauty and architecture and art and fashion.

GW: Would you consider Pier 59 to be the most technologically advanced photo studio in the world?

FP: It is definitely the largest studio complex in the world and we are extremely technologically advanced, but one can never say we are the most technologically advanced because technology advances so fast that it is in continuous evolution. But we always do our very best to be at the cutting edge of that cycle—absolutely.

GW: Recall some of the more memorable moments at Pier 59.

FP: There have been so many moments. I can remember the volcano being built for a Britney Spears album cover shoot; or the perfect replica of the Oval Office of the White House for another shoot; or Peter Beard shooting with an elephant on another occasion. We have had many scenarios—models with tigers and all that. We constantly challenge ourselves to make sure whatever the request, whatever the imagination—that we can meet their demands.

GW: And I consider the commissary at Pier 59 just the very best. Not even Condé Nast or Goldman Sachs has a chicer, more exclusive commissary than the one at Pier 59.

FP: We take great pride in everything here, including the food.

{ JACKIE COLLINS }

JULY 2008

I t was the night of September 19, 2015, at precisely 11:51 p.m., when I walked into Omar's and the boîte's legendary maître d' and conspiracy theorist, Clifton "Querelle" Turner, first told me that my friend Jackie Collins had died. I looked at him, as he stroked his muskrat scruff that he considers a goatee, and laughed, thinking it was another one of his conspiracy theories. But it was true. It was shocking because only twelve days before, Jackie and I emailed, and I told her I couldn't wait for her to host my book party in Beverly Hills. She was fearless, stoic, and a woman of immense strength till the very end.

I will never forget the first time I met her. It was over lunch at Le Cirque. We sat at the best table in the restaurant and spent the next three hours having the most fun-filled tête-à-tête ever! I remember, too, that the scent she wore that day was as intoxicating as she was, this real housewife of Hollywood. "It is a mishmash of Christian Dior's Poison" were her precise words to me. And what a career! The prolific novelist has penned more than thirty books that have sold in excess of five hundred million copies. Lunch at Le Cirque was a rollicking affair filled with great mirth and gossip—quite unforgettable. The notoriously private queen of raunch fiction had no choice but to rip aside the veil covering her private life—but only for GW!

GW: Hi, darling!

JC: How are you, my sweetheart? We should be sitting in some fabulous restaurant having a highly expensive lunch. Discussing everybody and everything.

GW: I tell everyone that the most memorable lunch I've ever had was in the company of Jackie Collins. We had the most rollicking time. Have you been thinking about me?

JC: I think about you every morning.

GW: Yeah, right. You are on your toes, honey. In the morning you think of me as you slab a pound of La Mer wrinkle cream all over your haggard face.

JC: I don't like La Mer. The other one, the Swiss one— what's it called? It's in a blue pot.

GW: Is it true you write all of your books in longhand?

JC: I do, sweetheart, and I still do, and then I have them all leather-bound at the end, which I love.

GW: How many months does it usually take to tap out one of these steamy Jackie Collins novels?

JC: It takes me about nine months. It's like having a baby. Then you want to go out and give it a good start in life.

GW: I read a chapter of your new one and I wanted to have an angina. The book opens as the character looks at her nude image in a full-length mirror—readying herself for a $30,000-an-hour sexual encounter with a fifty-year-old.

JC: It's totally based on truth.

GW: A Jackie Collins novel knows no bounds.

JC: Then the character of Caroline came to mind because of what goes on in Washington with the politicians, who are actually more randy than actors. I remember being at a dinner before Clinton was elected and one of his aides was there and he said to me, "He's going to be a great president, but we have one problem." I said, "What problem is that?" He said, "The zipper problem." I couldn't make that up. And it turned out to be the zipper problem.

GW: You're now almost seventy-two years old. Are you still fucking?

JC: Whenever I want to.

GW: Men are always fucking, so I assume you still are.

JC: Well, of course, aren't you?

GW: Honey, I haven't got laid in so long, I need to go back to Russia. I heard you were giving head to the boys' wrestling coach in his office.

JC: I didn't have any boys at school, unfortunately. I wish

I had. I should have gone to school in America. It was an all-girls school.

GW: Any bouts of lesbiana in your past? Can you give me a little hint, if it's going to be in your memoir?

JC: Well, I did go to an all-girls school. Need I say more?

GW: Well, all of her stories are about the incredible, edible labia. So I assume now that Jackie Collins has dabbled in forbidden fruit!

JC: Honey, I've dabbled in everything. Are you on Twitter?

GW: Nope. Twitter's like Clint Eastwood—it's for twits. Why does GW have the distinct feel that you and your sister, Joan Collins, are hardly close?

JC: That is so ridiculous. She was just here. She buys the English papers when she's here and sends them over to me every day. That's how close we are. She's great. I love my sister. When you have two powerful women and they're both successful, the media love the fact that they can create some kind of controversy between them. But she's coming to me for Christmas. I shall cook Christmas lunch for twenty-three people. When I built my house, I built a huge kitchen just for Christmas lunch.

GW: Who would have thought that Jackie Collins is the mother of three kids? That in itself is shocking. What do they do?

JC: One of them is a writer. She writes children's books. The other two work with children. They like to stay out of the limelight. They're not Hollywood kids. They're never those kids who are, "Here's a photo session of me and Mummy," forget about that. They have their own personalities.

GW: The first time I met your sister, Joan, she insisted I meet her at a Starbucks on Fifty-seventh Street.

JC: That doesn't sound like her at all!

GW: I couldn't believe it! Sure enough, she strolled into that Starbucks in a slate-gray Giorgio Armani suit that afternoon and no one batted an eye.

JC: I love it. That's New York. You know I wrote the original book *The Stud*, and she starred in the movie playing Fontaine. She was amazing in the movie. Naked on a swing!

GW: How do you keep writer's block at bay?

JC: I don't ever have writer's block—I have "getting to the desk block," which is a whole different thing. You get up in the morning and you think, I really should get to my desk immediately. But first I shall walk the dog, I shall go to the fridge, I shall make eggs for breakfast—not that I eat breakfast, I don't—do this, that, and the other, make ten phone calls, and then once I'm at my desk I just start writing and it flows. I love creating characters. I grew up reading Dickens and Harold Robbins.

GW: That's what makes you such a downer. What's your favorite quote from the Bible?

JC: I don't read the Bible.

GW: You've never read a chapter of the Bible?

JC: I don't read the Bible; I'm not a religious person. I'm a Buddhist, a hovering Buddhist. I don't read the Bible, but I feel that religion is responsible for all the ills in the world.

{ TAMARA MELLON }

JANUARY 2017

Tamara Mellon is my epitome of the driven, über-posh, intellectually advanced, well-bred English woman. The fact that she engineered a legendary fashion brand is the icing on the cake . . . well, maybe.

Tamara Mellon cofounded Jimmy Choo, the luxe shoe company in 1996, and without question the success of that fashion accessory cements her claim to being one of the most dynamic and influential fashion personalities of the last fifty years.

She departed Jimmy Choo in 2011 in a huff, and the trials and the tribulations that have ensued are now the stuff of legend. The vicious Sturm und Drang that unfolded after divesting her from that fashion accessory brand continues well into 2017. The mudslinging and the lawsuits, the back and forth recriminations with her former partners and investors at

Jimmy Choo are beyond travesty. We haven't seen such madness since the days of the blitzkrieg.

The continued drama would have devastated mere mortals. But Tamara Mellon is no mere mortal. She has fought off the sharks, her detractors, whose only goal, it seems, is to continue to spur her demise. She sought to reinvent herself and create a new fashion focus, TMB [Tamara Mellon Brand], in 2013, only to be forced into bankruptcy in 2016 by the continuous subterfuge and alleged nefarious tactics of her former partners, now diabolical enemies.

"After parting ways, I worked tirelessly to build a groundbreaking new brand. But the inappropriate actions of my former company threw a wrench in our ability to move forward. The vicious, irresponsible, and soulless liars and fraudsters" are still chomping at her heels.

But moving forward is exactly what Tamara Mellon continues to do. Cleopatra would have been proud. . . .

GW: First came Manolo Blahnik; then came Tamara Mellon for Jimmy Choo. Then there was a snafu and Christian Louboutin swooped in and stepped in your shoes, for want of better words, and stole your thunder. Now you are back with a major comeback all under your name Tamara Mellon Brand. Give us the backstory of what led to all this? What led to that chasm with Jimmy Choo?

TM: I sold the brand in 2011 and I think it was very hard for me to come to grips with selling the majority of my business and then realizing that I had suddenly become a guest in my own house, so I had to get out. I saw things being done to the product that I would never have done myself. For them it was just about the profit margins and not the long-term viability of the business. And as a founder I cared about different things, so for me it was very hard to stand by and just let that happen. So I really didn't before that have any experience with investors and the like. And by the time I came to realize what this was all going to be, it was too late. They were already too far in. And you were right, back in the beginning there was really only one brand and that was Manolo Blahnik. And as you probably do know, I started off as a glossy magazine editor.

GW: How did the idea of creating Jimmy Choo dawn on you?

TM: In those days, of the early nineties and as an editor, I just got bored shooting the same brand [Manolo Blahnik]. And we would go down to Jimmy's studio on the East End of London. We would get him to make some shoes for us. I would say to him, for instance, "Hey, Jimmy I need a pair of Grecian sandals and I want it flat with lattice leather straps," and he would make them. I wasn't the only editor who would do this. And of course, we would photograph the shoes and give him credit in *Vogue*. And then people started asking where they could get the shoes. And there was nowhere to actually get them! So naturally I thought, Wow, what a great platform to start a business. And that is how it all began in 1996. So I went to Jimmy and I said, "Let's build a business."

GW: Wow! What balls.

TM: I mean, literally where the shop was located, basically this disused garage in the East End of London that was dangerous. We would go there and park our cars behind gates that had to be padlocked. That is how dangerous it was. And that is where he would be making these shoes. And so I said, "Jimmy you help design the collection and I will raise the money and open the stores and find the factories. I will do the whole operation." I actually borrowed money from my father. I borrowed one hundred and fifty thousand dollars from my dad, because nobody would put money in because I had no track record and neither did Jimmy. And then I flew to Italy and found factories.

GW: Really, seriously, when I saw having balls, this was so bold and audacious, all the things you are telling me!

TM: I don't know how I did it. When I think back, and what I did, if I had really thought about what I was doing I would probably have been scared to do it. So I went to Italy with the book, I had a listing of factories, and just basically knocked on doors asking, Can you make these shoes? And then we opened the first store, the size of a coffee table, on Jermyn Street. And it became so popular. And then it sort of evolved to my designing the shoes and Jimmy making them. That was really his forte. Jimmy had that technical skill of making the shoes but he didn't have the creative flair to design the collection.

GW: And what is the shoe design process all about for Tamara Mellon?

TM: Though I am not the genius sketcher, say of Manolo [Blahnik], I work differently. I work from images and mood boards and vintage shopping. I have it in my head and come up with the ideas via images. And so then 1997 was a benchmark year for the brand. It was the breakout collection when we did the shoes with the feathers on them, and Carrie Bradshaw [Sarah Jessica Parker] went on to wail in *Sex and the City*, "I lost my Choo! I lost my Choo!" And I remember when we had a sale that year, there was a line around the block. The women were going crazy, pushing and screaming to get in.

GW: And who was the first major brick-and-mortar to carry the brand in the United States?

TM: It was Saks Fifth Avenue.

GW: Then business boomed and then what?

TM: In 2001, Jimmy decided to sell his shares and that is how private equity got into my business. Jimmy sold his shares to private equity and none of them ever put money into the business. All they did was buy shares. The only way we grew the business was from what we generated from cash flow. It was a constant musical chairs of private equity companies coming into the business, and therein lay my frustration. It was exhausting. And so in 2011 when Lever Luxe bought the business I sold my equity. It was all just more of the same. So I made some money and sold my shares.

GW: What do you think of the brand Jimmy Choo today?

TM: I don't know! I don't even look at it. And that is why I wrote a book [*In My Shoes*], I closed that chapter and it was quite cathartic.

GW: Who is the Tamara Mellon woman?

TM: She definitely has a seventies side to her, considering it is my favorite decade. But she is also an independent, free-spirited woman. She is a woman in charge of her own life. She is, of course, fashionable and loves luxury. She is really glamorous but not over-made or overdone. She is natural. She epitomizes natural glamor.

GW: And who were your fashion icons as a teenager?

TM: Halston, Gucci, and Fiorucci . . .

GW: Just ask the girls of Sister Sledge!

TM: I loved Ted Lapidus, Elsa Peretti, too.

GW: And I hear you also went to finishing school in Switzerland. The very same finishing school that Princess Diana attended.

TM: Yes. It was a girl's finishing school in Switzerland that Diana attended a few years before I did. It was just us sixty girls on the outskirts of Gstaad, where Le Rosey was. And it was in a little village called Route Mont. The school was called Vida Minette Institute Alpine. It was so old-fashioned. We basically learnt how to get in and out of sports cars and how to set a table and how to entertain. We learnt French. It was basically learning how to cook, ski, and speak French! Unbelievable, right?

GW: And then, of course, your crazy marriage to Matthew Mellon. . . . Why did you leave him? Sex, drugs, and rock 'n' roll? You had to have known that before you married him! That was a disaster.

TM: I know, but I have a beautiful daughter that was worth it.

GW: But who names their daughter Araminthe?

TM: Call her "Minty." Araminthe is actually a very old English name and you find Araminthe around Oxfordshire, and we got married at Blenheim Palace so it seemed right. And I just love the name Minty Mellon.

GW: How did you meet crazy Matthew Mellon?

TM: We met through mutual friends and when I met Matthew he was sober. I had been sober for twenty years and he had been sober for three years when I met him. So I thought he was going to stay sober. I did, and he didn't, and that was the breakdown of our marriage. He never had anything to do with the business.

GW: For a while there, what I call "Fugly" shoes were suddenly the norm. Those hideous platform shoes, you know like the grotesque shoes that Sofía Vergara likes to wear. You know what I mean.

TM: Yes, I know, we go through strange cycles. It got to the point where I couldn't bear to see another crazy high platform shoe and the way women were wearing them. I think we are definitely out of that cycle now.

GW: Tell that to Sofía Vergara!

TM: It's swung now to a much lower heel and so the timing could not be more perfect for Tamara Mellon Brand.

GW: Manolo or Louboutin? Who is more genius and why?

TM: You know, the market was so different than when we started Jimmy Choo. Back then, there was no one, there was only Manolo. Today the market is flooded with a lot of talented people. I think Aquazzura is really talented and Gianvito Rossi is really talented. He is the son of Sergio Rossi.

GW: What about Chloe Gosselin? She is a major emerging new talent. Dare I say that she could be "the next Tamara Mellon"?

TM: I think she is a great talent. I don't know her personally at all. We have never met. But as I said, the market is flooded with a lot of talented people these days.

GW: Before we go, tell us about your new boyfriend.

TM: It's not really new. It's been four years already.

GW: Yet how is it that we never see any paparazzi shots of Mike Ovitz and Tamara Mellon anywhere! It's as if this is the most reclusive couple in America. Even worse than David Bowie and Iman—who we never, ever see in public together. You guys are almost on that level. We never see or hear of Mike Ovitz and Tamara Mellon appearing or being seen anywhere. Not even in Cannes at Elton John's AIDS Foundation charity gala on whose board you also sit.

TM: We didn't go to Cannes this year. And I guess "the paps" are not around any of the places that we go.

GW: How do you both keep this relationship so quiet?

TM: I guess, you know, ahhmm . . . I guess, we sort of, you know . . . I guess they are just not around where we are. We do dinners and we do art auctions. We just go about our lives pretty much like any other couple, really.

GW: What is he like, Mike Ovitz? GW needs to meet Mike Ovitz. He needs a Talent Manager guru.

TM: But he is no longer in the Hollywood business anymore. He left that a long time ago. He's done with that. He is now involved in the tech world making investments in tech-based startups.

GW: So he is not a recluse?

TM: He is not a recluse at all.

GW: Is it the best relationship you have ever had?

TM: It is the best relationship I have ever had. I love being with a really smart man. He is incredibly intelligent, and when I look at all the things he does today I am just amazed. He got into the tech business way back in the early nineties, way before anyone else did. He realized this was the future. He has always been so far ahead of anyone in everything he does. And he has one of the most amazing art collections in the world.

GW: Mike Ovitz ought to know that he is lucky to have a cool chick like you in his life, Tamara Mellon. And GW thanks you!

{ RÉGINE }

R égine Choukroun was the original Queen of the Night. Before there was Elaine—for sure before there was Susanne Bartsch—there was the one and only Régine, who all her life was always the first to claim that it was she who invented the notion of the discotheque.

Even if that is not true, at one time she actually did own nineteen nightclubs across the chicest cities and ports on the globe. When I interviewed Régine in 1996, she was in the midst of writing her memoirs. We met of course over a jeroboam of Taittinger champagne, at the Park Avenue Manhattan outpost of her eponymous disco, Regine [*sic*].

GW: How was your summer in Saint-Tropez, Queen Régine?

R: I am finishing writing my book about the clubs. It

will be a very serious book, but, of course, we will talk about the people who came to these clubs. It will be out next year.

GW: Queen Régine, what happened when you and your son, Lionel Rotcage, were arrested on an American Airlines flight after he lit a cigarette?

R: We were in business class, and let me tell you, for seven years I traveled with American Airlines. So I am known. I'm a VIP. They bring me to the plane. They make a lot of "chichi."

GW: But then if you dare to express your feelings, they [flight attendants] think you are threatening them.

R: Exactly! Now, my son has a little girl, and she wanted to use the toilet, so he stood up with his daughter and took her. Now he's in the smoking section. And he decided to have a cigarette. One second after, a steward rapped him on the shoulder and said, "Kill that!" Lionel told him he was just waiting for his daughter in the toilet. But he runs back and gets the purser, a very aggressive woman. So he put out the cigarette and gave it to her. I think she took it badly. And she said, "The captain says if you light another cigarette he will land the plane." Lionel told her he understood and she should stop threatening him. She left, goes to the captain. He comes back and says, "You've just threatened my crew." My son told him it was the reverse. The captain said he didn't want to hear it and he was going to land the plane. He was hysterical. It was a nightmare. They said they were landing in Boston to refuel. They were lying. They put us in jail.

GW: They put Régine in a filthy prison cell?!

R: Exactly. We were fingerprinted. They took pictures like we were criminals.

GW: Tell me a little about Régine Choukroun's life?

R: I was born in Belgium and I grew up in Paris. And I decided very early to become somebody very famous. You know, I invented the discotheque. I invented the colored lighting for the disco. I made the twist very famous.

GW: What was your first club?

R: Chez Régine in 1957. In 1962, I opened New Jimmy's. In 1973, I opened in Brazil; in '76, New York. Then nineteen clubs on three continents.

GW: How many clubs are still open?

R: Six. I'm also a singer, an actress.

GW: And a drama queen who still loves the nightlife.

R: I still love to dance until six in the morning.

GW: Did you really teach the Duke of Windsor how to do the twist?

R: Yes. One night I received a call from the personal secretary of the Duke and Duchess of Windsor. One hour later they arrived at the café. And that was the beginning of a very, very strong friendship.

GW: Who was one of the first celebrities you ever met?

R: [Porfirio] Rubirosa.

GW: Did you ever see that legendary "thing"?

R: Yes. [Laughs.]

GW: Was it as big as legend has it?

R: Absolutely. But that was not his first quality. He was a very fabulous man, and a very good friend.

GW: Any great diva has to be a bit of an egomaniac. So I suppose you are one, too.

R: No, no. I don't have a big ego. I'm the only diva without a big ego.

GW: Régine has seen much. What keeps her interested in life?

R: I'm a very curious person. I think every morning is a new adventure—and every night also.

Donatella
Versace

{DONATELLA VERSACE}

MARCH 1994

There was not a better, grander, more fabulous time to be in the company of the Versace clan in Miami Beach than over the Christmas season of 1993, which is when this GW Q&A with Donatella Versace was conducted for *Vanity Fair*. I got to the huge, over-wrought-iron gate of Casa Casuarina that sunny, already sweltering Miami afternoon and was immediately welcomed. We proceeded to the dining room and sat for a hearty and healthy lunch of veal and mixed greens. Gianni was at the head of the table and Donatella was at the other. Gianni was dishing on Elton, Anna Wintour, Linda Evangelista, and Princess Diana, and I could barely keep my jaw in check! But I just have to tell you this priceless anecdote that Gianni revealed that day about Princess Diana. Gianni told the table, to uproarious laughter, a story I have no doubt he probably told a thousand times before and after. Gianni said that he remembered the first time he

sent a rack of Versace's finest couture over to Kensington Palace. "So she calls me on the phone," Gianni said, "thanking
me profusely but insisting that she had to write a check to pay"
for the Versace couture frocks. "She would not take no for an
answer." And a day later, HRH the Princess of Wales had her
envoy deliver an envelope to Atelier Versace's showroom in
London. "It was a personal check for one hundred pounds,
which I had framed and placed in my office." I just about
spewed my champagne across the room into Paul Beck's face
[Donatella's husband]. That was Gianni Versace for you. And
ooh, how much I miss him! After that unforgettable lunch,
Donatella and GW retreated to her private quarters. We sat
on the bed in her gargantuan bedroom as she chain-smoked a
pack of Marlboro Red cigarettes and we conducted this GW
Q&A Hall of Fame classic!

GW: They say that Donatella is the muse of Gianni Versace?
What exactly is your role in the house?

DV: It's a family company, so my first role is sister and
friend to my brothers, Gianni and Santo. We have no
yes-men around, and that is very important. I do the
accessories, the children's line, the lingerie line, and
the Versus Collection. But my main role is working
with Gianni twenty-four hours a day. I'm on the case
all day long. I drive him crazy, but I think a designer
can be greater with a feminine opinion.

GW: What is a typical day for you?

DV: I have breakfast with my family, and then I leave the
house at 7:45 and work out until 9:30. Then, I take

a shower and go up to my office. I say good morning to Gianni, and we start the day, first looking at fabrics and sketches, making modifications and alterations. Then I do my own things. At 1:00 p.m. every day, Gianni and I meet for lunch at his house. Then we go back to work. At night I go home, watch cartoons, put the children to bed, and after that, if I have to do something else, I'll do it. I take care to spend time with the children.

GW: The Versace name continues to blaze. You are now ensconced here at Casa Casuarina, and when the Versace Jeans Couture boutique opened in South Beach, it did ten thousand dollars' worth of business in the first hour!

DV: We are very excited, and we've put so much effort into this because it's not easy to carry on all this and to keep pushing forward. It is a risk all the time, but we like that.

GW: The House of Versace is known for innovation. After all, it is credited with the supermodel phenomenon.

DV: That's true. We put Cindy Crawford, Linda Evangelista, and Christy Turlington on the runway, and pretty soon they were big.

GW: Which girls do you think are next in line for the title of world supermodel?

DV: I love Bridget Hall. I think that she is going to be a big star. And I like Amber Valletta a lot.

GW: You have a gorgeous husband, Paul Beck, and two beautiful children, Allegra and Daniel. From the day they were born, they were probably dressed in Versace.

DV: They were always dressed in Versace. Allegra, she was out in the park at one month old in a whole outfit full of lace, everything embroidered.

GW: Allegra must be a real little princess!

DV: She likes to wear good clothes, but she is not spoiled. I was told as a little girl to understand the value of everything, so I was not too spoiled either.

GW: Do you realize that you are a very important woman in the world of fashion?

DV: No. I don't look at myself as important in the world.

GW: You are, however, very much into the rock 'n' roll scene.

DV: I do know a lot of rock stars. The first one I met was Elton John, and now we are very close. Now one of my favorite rock-star friends is Axl Rose. People think Axl is a troublemaker, but he is such a sweet person. And then of course I see a lot of Sting. He and Trudie have three children the same age as mine, so we see them a lot.

GW: So when is Gianni going to introduce a fragrance called Donatella?

DV: That's a good question, because Gianni wants to do that! We are considering doing a new fragrance, and he wants to call it Donatella.

GW: Tell me another project the house of Versace has in the pipeline that has never been revealed?

DV: We want to do something pretty different in the new

year, especially regarding the fashion shows and the way the fashion shows are done. The problem is we have so many people copying us, and stuff arriving in shops before we can. So we have to look at a totally new way to present the collection. It will be a big difference for sure.

{ KENNETH JAY LANE }

NOVEMBER 1996

enneth Jay Lane was the costume jeweler to crowned heads, first ladies, and style goddesses all over the world. Kenny Lane, as his many moneyed and important clients and friends knew him, single-handedly made fake jewels haute joaillerie. His memoir, *Faking It*, remains one of the most hilarious and profound by any fashion royal. . . .

GW: When did Kenny Lane discover his aesthetic to create jewelry?

KJL: I guess I'd seen a picture of Mae West in a magazine. She was my ideal. In 1962, I did my first collection, licensed by [Arnold] Scaasi.

GW: Your new book, *Faking It*, isn't as bitchy and dishy as one would have expected.

KJL: Why be bitchy? Everyone has always been good to me. So I had nothing to dish. I have no complaints. The only memories I have are pleasant things.

GW: In the book you call yourself "part pugilist, part genius, part magician, part wizard, part snake charmer." What you forgot to say was that you are also high society's favorite walker.

KJL: Oh good God! Yes, I can walk, I can dance. I own several tuxedos. But I don't consider going to the movies with Nan Kempner walking. I regard that as sitting.

GW: Your favorite saying throughout the book is "I was very fortunate. . . ." But what do you think has been your greatest fortune?

KJL: Probably having the right philosophy about life. Positive thinking. I learned a great deal from Diana Vreeland. She had a wonderful philosophy. She always said, "Always give ideas away," because under every idea there is another waiting to be born. I mean, I have had many ups and downs. But you just can't complain. You just have to go on. So you lose a half-million dollars here, a half-million dollars there. Tomorrow is another day.

GW: Marilyn Monroe was the big one that got away. She was never one of your clients.

KJL: No, but I did make shoes for her. I knew her and I even went out with her. How about that? I was her walker. When she was married to Arthur Miller, Norman

Norell asked me to make a special last for Marilyn. She had a very high instep, and she loved a super-high heel like Marlene Dietrich's so that her foot went like a Vargas girl's. I personally took those shoes to her apartment at 444 East 57th Street. She was adorable, so funny. And she talked exactly like she did in her films. I remember going shopping with her once to look for a bed. She had a beret on to cover up her hair and huge sunglasses. Nobody looked at her, nobody. She was so annoyed, so she took the beret off. I took her once to something at the Waldorf. She asked me to go with her because Arthur Miller hated those things. And she hated it, too, in a way, because people used to grab at her. People would grab buttons off her clothes, and that sort of thing. It took her hours and hours to get dressed. I'd be talking to Arthur and watching something on television. Then finally she would arrive looking like something you've never seen. I remember a red lace dress by Norell. Just over the knees, black stockings, bright red shoes. And her maid would wrap the little stole around her. And she would say, "Be careful, don't damage the merchandise." By the time we got to the Waldorf, it was over with. We walk into P.J.'s, Marilyn looking unbelievable. It was a written rule in P.J.'s: no autographs, no staring. But when she walked in, conversation stopped.

GW: My favorite Kenny Lane moment is watching you finger a caviar bowl at this fabulous Beverly Hills party hosted by Marvin and Barbara Davis. It was the funniest, realest moment of the entire evening.

KJL: [Laughs] I eat my salad too with my fingers. I love eating with my fingers.

GW: Is your life an open book, Kenneth Jay Lane?

KJL: Yeah, pretty much. I have no secret life, unfortunately.

{ MR. BLACKWELL }

MAY 1995

E veryone these days has an InstaReady Best Dressed List. Or as Dame Helen Mirren so succinctly quipped, "Ignore anyone who judges the way you look, especially . . . some anonymous miserable creep, lurking on the Internet. . . ."

Mr. Blackwell was no creep, that's for sure. Back in the day, the irrepressible Mr. Blackwell was the creator and gatekeeper of his annual "Ten Worst Dressed Women List." Back then he was the fashion Gorgon, feared and loathed by the world's biggest personalities, who, despite it all, still had to seek and have a peek at Mr. Blackwell's must-read compendium. Were he here now, one can only ponder what Mr. Blackwell would have to say about Rihanna and Lady Gaga.

GW: Considering you are the curmudgeon of fashion, Mr. B, your new autobiography, *From Rags to Bitches*, could not be more aptly titled.

Mr. B: Correct. And that includes both the gender and the attitude.

GW: Ever since 1960, you've compiled your worst dressed list. How do you go about it?

Mr. B: It's so simple. I just take a look, like any other human being does. They go home and get a little nauseous and call up the neighbor and gossip about it. The difference between those people, who are really more evil because they are not open and out about it, and me is that I come right out and say exactly what *they* are thinking.

GW: Now Madonna, for example, would probably spit in your face if you ever went near her. You once called her "the queen of pretense and peroxide."

Mr. B: That's exactly what she is!

GW: And you once called Ivana Trump "a cross between Bridget Bardot and Lassie."

Mr. B: That was only one year. She has redeemed herself in a hundred ways.

GW: And Cher "a bag of tattooed bones in a sequined slingshot."

Mr. B: Well, I was being kind! That was the kindest thing I ever said.

GW: I find it interesting that your own personal style favors European design: Brioni, Armani, and the masculine glamor of my favorite, Hugo Boss.

Mr. B: I love Hugo Boss. I like the attitude of European clothes.

GW: Now, Mr. B, you have had about a dozen face-lifts. Am I correct?

Mr. B: No!!!

GW: But your face is tighter than a trampoline!

Mr. B: It is not! My face is very natural looking. I think my surgeon is terrific.

GW: Why does Mr. B hate John Fairchild, the publisher of *Women's Wear Daily*? Why does that name drive him to such venom?

Mr. B: Well, I don't think that man is fair. He has said, "I don't intend to report fashion. I intend to dictate it." And he said anyone who disagreed with him he would destroy. I called him and said, "It's too late, you can't destroy me." And then I asked him to send me snapshots of his wife wearing the clothes he was front-paging in his newspaper. And you know what the answer was? He slammed the phone down on me.

GW: One of the greatest revelations of *From Rags to Bitches* is your love affairs with Tyrone Power, Cary Grant, and his boyfriend Randolph Scott. But you don't give any details. These affairs warranted their own chapters!

Mr. B: The details aren't important. This isn't a porno book! I was pleased that I became part of unions, part of relationships that gave me confidence, that made me feel wanted. I gave them, those people—and there were many more—the same feeling of joy, of confidence, of need.

GW: I was trying to imagine myself being in that beach house that Cary Grant shared with Randolph Scott.

Mr. B: What was so wonderful was, here were two terrific people who took me in. What those two did for me at that time of my life—I would have no idea how to repay them.

GW: My favorite factoid from your book is that when Howard Hughes went to Chasen's, he wore mud-caked tennis shoes.

Mr. B: Well, yes, that was Howard.

GW: Whatever happened to your fragrances, Mr. Blackwell number ten and Mr. Blackwell number eleven?

Mr. B: I was the first couturier in America to come out with his own perfume.

GW: The first?

Mr. B: Yes, I was the first.

GW: And that's a fact no one can take away from you, not even Mr. Fairchild.

Mr. B: George, I have no regrets, and no apologies for anything I've ever done!

Graydon Carter

Dana Barr

{ G R A Y D O N   C A R T E R **}**

SEPTEMBER 2013

I have never been more nervous before an interview than I was before this audience with Graydon Carter. He is my boss after all, and who wants to interview his boss? This interview was the bright idea of another brilliant editor in chief, Brandusa Niro of the must-read New York Fashion Week glossy called the *Daily Front Row.* And so one fine day in 2013 I went to sit with GC for the record. I never allow a third party to sit in on my interviews, but I certainly was not going to say no to *Vanity Fair* PR queen Beth Kseniak, who insisted on sitting in on this GW Q&A.

GW: Twenty incredible years and counting, GC—and hopefully twenty more at least! This interview will be an instant classic. Let us start with fashion: What is it you enjoy so much about a Carolina Herrera show, where you are a front-row perennial season after season?

GC: I go to Carolina's show because of Carolina herself. She is a dear old friend and I happen to love my wife in her clothes. Plus, I get to see Reinaldo play the role of majordomo, in terms of seating everybody and ordering people like me around. Reinaldo, in fact, would make a perfect maître d'. If he gets offers from this suggestion, I would appreciate a headhunting fee.

GW: What other shows are a must-see for you?

GC: I also like going to Ralph Lauren and Diane von Furstenberg and any others I can squeeze in during the week.

GW: What year did you move to New York, and from where, GC?

GC: In 1978 from Ottawa, Canada.

GW: Ah yes, Ottawa—the most boring city in the world.

GC: If you say so, GW. I'll tell you, it was a pretty wonderful place to grow up. I left there at the end of the summer of '78 to work for *Time*.

GW: As a ten-year-old growing up in provincial Ottawa, what did you dream of becoming?

GC: Well, most of all, I grew up wanting to be a New Yorker.

GW: Even then?

GC: Pretty much. And later, when I was in my teens, I envisioned myself as a painter or playwright.

GW: Growing up in provincial Ottawa, did you have Sitka spruce and red cedar trees in your backyard?

GC: Yes, it's a very woody, snow-filled part of the country. We had a skating rink out back.

GW: How glamorous! You used to be E. Graydon Carter. What does the initial stand for?

GC: Edward—but my father went by Edward. I was always Graydon, or Gray, to my family and most of my friends.

GW: And who is your favorite tailor, GC?

GC: Anderson and Sheppard, ever since I could afford them in my early thirties.

GW: And your favorite author?

GC: P. G. Wodehouse.

GW: Favorite poet?

GC: W. H. Auden.

GW: Favorite pop star?

GC: That would have to be Mick Jagger.

GW: And your favorite movie of all time would be?

GC: *The Philadelphia Story*—it's a crisp, brilliant film. I do love the fact that Jimmy Stewart plays a reporter for a magazine called *Spy*. It was one of the influences for us choosing that name for our magazine in the mid-eighties.

GW: Where does GC get his signature coif styled and feathered, and how often?

GC: A friend from Connecticut by the name of Craig Linley comes over to my house every two to three weeks. He sometimes cuts my kids' hair, too.

GW: And what will be the title of your memoirs?

GC: Friends have suggested *Magna Carter*—oh God. I was thinking more along the lines of *Do I Have to Dial 9 to Get Out of Here?*

GW: Thank you for giving me a headline for this interview,

GC. I'm looking forward to reading those memoirs and having you recall in fullest detail your meeting Princess Diana for the first time at a reception hosted by you at the Serpentine Gallery. There are classic images from that event that will forever be part of your video hagiography. It was a seminal moment in her life. She wore that gorgeous, short, sexy black dress, and it was her first public appearance after Prince Charles declared he was guilty of infidelity. What do you remember from that night, GC?

GC: Yes, I think that dinner was the very same night that Prince Charles went on television to admit he was having an affair. But Diana kept her word and came to the dinner and was as lovely and as charming as ever. You know, she was a very normal person outside of all that. She did, however, seem emotionally brittle that evening, but she managed to maintain her composure. On that night and others, she expressed her fascination with Jackie Kennedy. I think she felt she was having the same experience with the Windsors that Jackie had had with the Kennedys.

GW: Where does GC like to venture when wanderlust takes hold?

GC: Europe. A new favorite spot is the Mayr spa in southern Austria. My wife and I went there in late November to sort of unwind and rejuvenate. The Herreras love it as well.

GW: There won't be any sweltering through the Serengeti for you, I suppose?

GC: Given the pressures of the magazine, I need access to the Internet and a constant flow of packages from FedEx. So the Serengeti will have to wait.

GW: You've never wanted to visit Bhutan or see a desert moon?

GC: I'd love to visit Bhutan. I don't know so much about the desert moon.

GW: How often does GC have lunch with Emperor Newhouse?

GC: Usually every ten days to two weeks.

GW: You know, GC, those of us who are fortunate enough to have the opportunity to work at your behest over all these years have come to realize just how brilliant you are. You are the modern master of pop-erature—pop literature—and you possess the most uncannily prescient mind. As you know, that is the gift all great editors possess, and you have it in spades.

GC: Thank you, GW, but you still won't be getting a raise.

GW: Since I have your undivided attention, I have to tell you, GC, that I was rather miffed after reading *Vanity Fair* number six hundred twenty-eight—the Kate Moss cover—and finding that the writer made no mention that it was I who first introduced Kate Moss to Johnny Depp. Naomi Campbell and Roy Liebenthal will attest to the fact that I introduced them in 1994 at the celebrity-infested boîte of the moment, Café Tabac. As you'll no doubt recall, Naomi and Kate were an inseparable duo back in those days. Naomi's nickname for Kate was "Wagon," for some reason. So Naomi and "Wagon" showed up to Café Tabac one night, and I instinctively grabbed Kate's hand and walked her over to Johnny Depp, who I didn't even know, and said, "Johnny, meet Kate." Who could have known that, because of me, they would go on to trash hotel rooms across the globe for years and years to come?

GC: I will make sure to alert the writer, James Fox, to what you have just declared, GW.

GW: Café Tabac was where all the supermodels went to let their hair down back then.

GC: Yes, I am aware of that.

GW: I'll also never forget the night at Tabac when Bono showed up with Christy Turlington and got her so sauced on shots of whiskey.

GC: That's quite a story, GW.

GW: Have you taken a private tour of One World Trade Center—the future home of Condé Nast—yet?

GC: I haven't been on a tour yet, but others here have. I've been to the office building beside it to see the view from our floor.

GW: Are you excited about the move downtown?

GC: I wasn't at first, but I'm excited now. People are saying it's going to be the twenty-first-century Rockefeller Center, and the more I go down there, the more I think they're right.

GW: But don't you think Ground Zero is haunted?

GC: If it's haunted, then the entire island of Manhattan is haunted.

GW: Croque-monsieur or Jamaican beef patty?

GC: Well, I've never eaten a Jamaican beef patty, but I do enjoy croque-monsieur.

GW: Edith Piaf or Charo?

GC: Piaf, of course, though I actually met Charo some thirty years ago when I was at *Time*.

GW: GW's favorite *Vanity Fair* Oscar-party moment ever was holding Gwynnie Paltrow's statuette the night she won. Remember that breathtaking pink Ralph Lauren gown she wore, GC? What are the most memorable moments for you over the many years of your world-famous party?

GC: I always take my children, and if there was ever one moment, it was the night they were introduced to Muhammad Ali. For some reason, it's always struck me as something they'll never forget.

GW: Any special surprises planned for this year?

GC: We always try to do something special. Of course, we also try to keep it a surprise for as long as possible.

GW: And who will have the distinct honor of sitting to your right at your über-exclusive pre-dinner party?

GC: Sitting to my right will probably be Fran Lebowitz. She usually draws the short straw.

GW: What do you always order at the Beatrice Inn?

GC: Well, we just changed the chef there, but I usually order the iceberg wedge and the chicken.

GW: Who is the new chef?

GC: That cannot be disclosed at this time, GW.

GW: Will there ever be an outpost of the Waverly Inn at the Wynn resort in sunny Las Vegas?

GC: A Waverly Wynn? No, I don't think so. We've been approached a number of times, but we're not sure how well it would translate.

GW: I don't believe that the lesbian woman is truly ready to be the next mayor of New York City. GW is backing Joe Lhota. Who would you like to see in Gracie Mansion?

GC: Aside from Ray Kelly and Christine Quinn? Fran—I think she'd make a fabulous mayor.

GW: And lastly, because it's *The Daily*, are you happy with your new creative director?

GC: Chris Dixon is a marvel and a joy to work with. Plus, he's Canadian, so he gets all my hockey jokes.

GW: Well, the reviews are unanimous: GC still rules! Thank you, my liege.

{ ROBERT EVANS }

APRIL 1999

T his is one of my all-time favorite interviews, for which I never did sit with the subject face to face. I was on vacation at the Half-Moon Resort in Montego Bay at the time with the only man I have ever been in love with—even to this day—one Manuel Esperito Santo. And oh, how much I wish he would come back to me. That said, we were on location in a stunning villa along the Caribbean Sea when the iconic Hollywood producer Robert Evans called from Los Angeles. We were on the phone for at least two hours—this after all is a true decades-long icon of show business, the visionary responsible for *The Godfather* and *Chinatown* amongst many other classics. To this day, his seminal memoir, *The Kid Stays in the Picture*, is a must-read. We talked for hours between my stuffing my face with jerk chicken. Every pun intended . . .

GW: Darling, you've been regaling GW with the declaration that he is only the second person in history, after Sherry Lansing, to see the seventeen-minute preview to the two-hour docudrama-movie work-in-progress based on your acclaimed autobiography, *The Kid Stays in the Picture*. I was absolutely mesmerized by that legendary Bob Evans lush purr!

RE: I've had that voice since I was eleven years old. I was a famous child actor on the radio.

GW: GW especially loved that sequence in the preview where you muse about being discovered in a nightclub by the legendary Darryl Zanuck. At which nightclub were you discovered by Zanuck?

RE: At El Morocco—the most famous nightclub at the time. I was doing the tango with Contessa Cristina Polizzi, and Albert, the captain at El Mo's, came over and said, "Mr. Zanuck would like to see you." So I went over to his table and Zanuck said, "Are you an actor, kid?" I said, "I'm not right now." He said, "We've been watching you dance for the last hour and a half. How would you like to star opposite Ava Gardner as the matador in *The Sun Also Rises*?" And that's how I got the part. I was the only actor ever under personal contract to Darryl Zanuck.

GW: Wow, that's absolutely queenious! You are still considered one of the longest-running studio heads in the history of Paramount Pictures. And it was about 1974 that you were considered the most powerful man in Hollywood.

RE: I would say from 1966 to 1976, but I don't wish to sound in any way self-serving, because a lot of other people contributed.

GW: But—my God—you haven't had a hit movie for years!

RE: I had a hit last year. *The Saint* was a big hit.

GW: The fact that it made one hundred million dollars overseas where people are starving for anything "made in America" does not make it a hit!

RE: Of the pictures I've made in this decade, the one I'm most proud of is *Jade*. Billy Friedkin is a wonderful director—I love working with him. I'm hoping that *The Out-of-Towners* will be a wonderful audience film.

GW: Well, you have Goldie Hawn. And, God knows, Steve Martin could sure use a hit just as much as you could!

RE: Well, I suppose everyone needs a hit. Of course, our business, George—and you know this—is run by the bottom line. My pictures, for that reason have not been bombs.

GW: That's a good point. GW gives kudos for that one! Now Bob, tell GW what was that two-week marriage to Catherine Oxenberg all about?

RE: Just that—two weeks.

GW: Yet another classic Bob Evans fiasco.

RE: No, it wasn't a fiasco. It was irrational behavior caused by my stroke. On May 6, 1998, I was proposing a toast to Wes Craven in my home. And it was like a bolt of lightning hit me, and I just fell to the floor. The doctors all but pronounced me dead. I saw the white light.

GW: That's amazing, Bob! But this fiasco marriage?!

RE: I've known Catherine for years. I have only nice things to say about her. I have gone through eight months of the most painful physical therapy any human could have. This must be retribution.

GW: The audio version of your memoir has been one of the most popular books on tape in Hollywood.

RE: I was reading the *New York Post*—this review which came out: "This may be the only audio book with a cult following . . . it's developed an evergreen status."

GW: Darling, it's all about the evergreen status! Robert Evans is a thoroughbred survivor. He is here forever!

{ JERRY HALL }

I was so ecstatic to be able to interview the fashion icon that will always be Jerry Hall. Not only was she one of the true original supermodels before the term even existed, she was a muse to so many men—including fashion designer Thierry Mugler and the rock-star icon Mick Jagger, for whom she would bear four children. Always one for a fabulous surprise, today she is happily married to the great Rupert Murdoch. And Jerry Hall's life could not be more idyllic.

On this day in early 1997, she was on the glorious West Indian island of Mustique, holidaying with her fabulous American fashion-designer friend and fellow fashion icon— Tommy Hilfiger. I could have spent hours more on the telephone just listening to that Texas meets Mayfair purr of hers . . . simply beguiling.

GW: You've been married into rock royalty for more than six years. And it's been . . .

JH: I can't talk to you for long because I'm late to get on this boat. We're going to a party at Tommy Hilfiger's.

GW: So I'm going to get right into it: you've been married to Mick Jagger for six years, and it's been . . . what?

JH: [Long pause] Well, we've been living together for twenty years, actually. And it's been exciting.

GW: Exciting and . . . ?

JH: Well, I think that's enough.

GW: Let's talk about those crazy days, Jerry Hall. Those days when you were a seventies supermodel.

JH: Well, I'm still modeling. I've got a three-year contract with Thierry Mugler's Angel perfume. And I did his show in Paris in January. And he's doing the clothes for my next movie, *The Prodigal Daughter*, in which I play a Mae West type. He's doing the most wonderful clothes.

GW: Fabulous!

JH: And I'm crazy flattered that I have been working with him for so long and he still likes me.

GW: But recall some anecdotes. What does Jerry Hall remember most from the Studio 54 era?

JH: I used to have so much fun with all the gang: Helmut Newton, Paloma Picasso, Salvador Dalí, Andy Warhol. We used to have such fun parties. Everybody was so into their art. They weren't so much into making money like now.

GW: Please! Andy was definitely into making money. What are you talking about? Warhol was all about money, Jerry. Please!

JH: Yeah, maybe. But Andy was so generous. I used to host for Andy Warhol's TV, and he used to pay me every week in art. I have a fabulous collection of Andy Warhol things. He paid me too much.

GW: Okay, you're right. He was a generous man, but by the same token he loved making money. What about those days with Anjelica Huston, Grace Jones, Iman? What if your daughter Elizabeth says, "Mama, I want to be a supermodel just like you"?

JH: I'd be thrilled because modeling is great. They're all shouting at me that we're going to miss the boat launch. So I'm going to have to go.

GW: But you can't leave yet darling. We have to talk about Jerry and Mick?

JH: I'm not talking about him.

GW: Jerry, just let me ask you this question: Why do you think so many Englishmen are such effete heterosexuals?

JH: I don't know. Maybe it's the school system. Or maybe it's in their genes.

GW: But Jerry, you must know. After all, you've been married to one of the biggest straight poofs GW has ever seen?

JH: [Laughs.] I don't know. Maybe Englishmen are more in touch with their feminine side.

GW: I hear the only reason you forgive Mick's indiscretions is that every time he's caught with his panties down, he has to buy you a bigger ruby than the last one.

JH: Where did you read that, the *National Enquirer*?

GW: No, darling! It's just something I thought of, actually.

JH: I don't want to talk about my personal life.

GW: But, Jerry, you must talk about how you keep the faith!

JH: I've got to go now.

GW: You're not going to talk about why you love your husband and won't divorce him?

JH: I think that's enough.

GW: Jerry, don't hang up!

JH: No. No way, man. I wish you good luck. Bye.

GW: Jerry! Jerry! Keep the faith, Jerry! Don't divorce Mick, even if he gets caught with his panties down again!

JH: [The telephone disconnects.]

{ACKNOWLEDGMENTS}

GW will forever acknowledge and revere the following: "Uncle" Noel Mignott, total class act and GW's greatest support system ever! The appreciated PCE (personal copy editor), Caroline Clouse; the GW digital guru, Kris Kicior; the indispensable aide-de-camp, Kris Ann Blagrove; the stalwart Dan Gilmore at *Vanity Fair* for all his help; Omar Hernandez and the incredible "family" at Omar's La Ranita, where *Anyone Who's Anyone* coalesced and gelled to perfection; without question, the legendary Emperor of Condé Nast, Si Newhouse; and my liege Graydon Carter, who granted GW the gig of a lifetime. For their patience and dedication my team at WME [William Morris Endeavor]—especially my amazing literary agent, Andy McNicol, and the sage counsel of Alicia Glekas Everett—and of course the peerless brilliance of my team at the iconic HarperCollins. GW is eternally grateful to all who continue to support and believe in this particular genius—that will include the PR majordomos: Brad Taylor, Richard Rubenstein, and Susan Magrino, whose help assures this book will become a leading bestseller with multiple printings and translations into many languages. . . .

GEORGE WAYNE was born in Kingston, Jamaica. He is a New York–based writer of twenty-six years who currently resides in Greenwich Village. His beat is celebrity culture and the whirl of fashion, music, and style. George conceived and launched his own avant-garde 'zine, *R.O.M.E.*, in 1986, and his career took off. He began as an associate editor at *Interview* magazine and later became the first contributing editor on the masthead of *Allure*. But his rise to recognition is attributed to his GW Q&As, which became a signature must-read of *Vanity Fair*, appearing regularly for twenty-two years.